DESERTING FROM THE CULTURE WARS

Editors: Maria Hlavajova and Sven Lütticken
Associate Editor: Wietske Maas
Managing Editor: Irene Calabuch Mirón
Copyediting: Colin Beckett
Proofreading: Mairead Case, Wietske Maas, Angelica Sgouros, and Aidan Wall
Design: Sean van den Steenhoven for LeftLoft

Cover features an image by Andreas Siekmann from the series *The Big 4ever*, 2020, developed for this publication.

This book was set in GT America and Minion Pro.

Distributed by:
The MIT Press
Massachusetts Institute of Technology
Cambridge, MA 02142

Library of Congress Control Number: 2020930210
ISBN: 978-0-262-53943-2

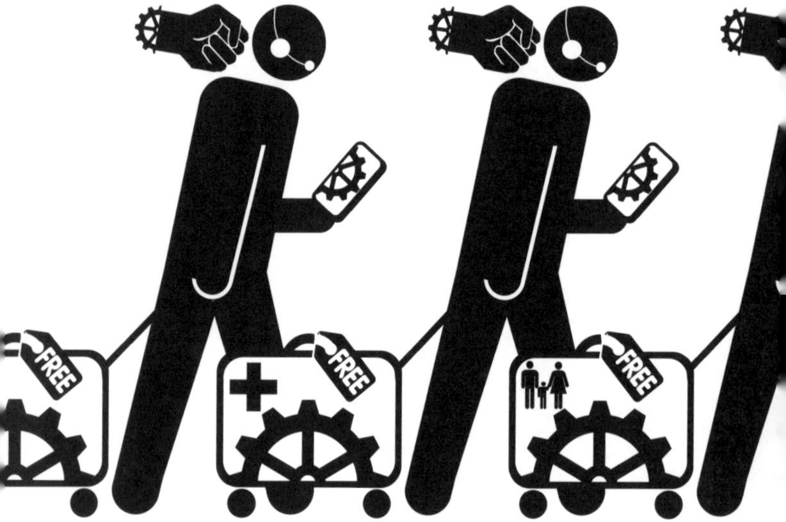
FREE
FREE
FREE

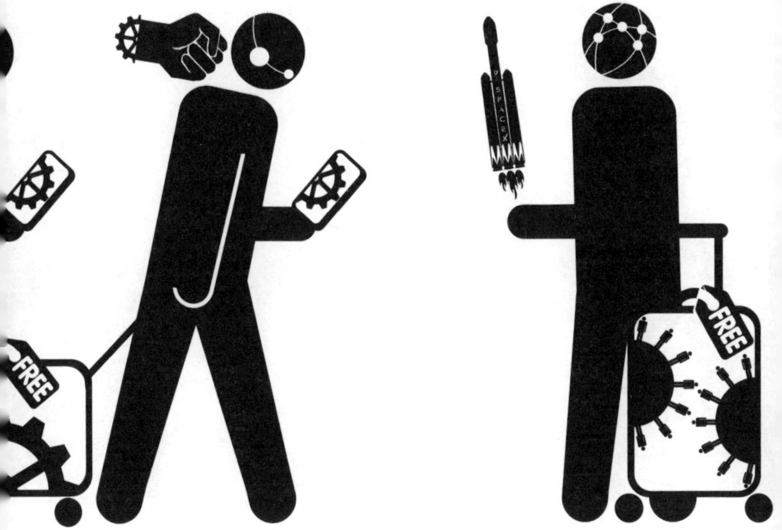

SPACEX
FREE
FREE

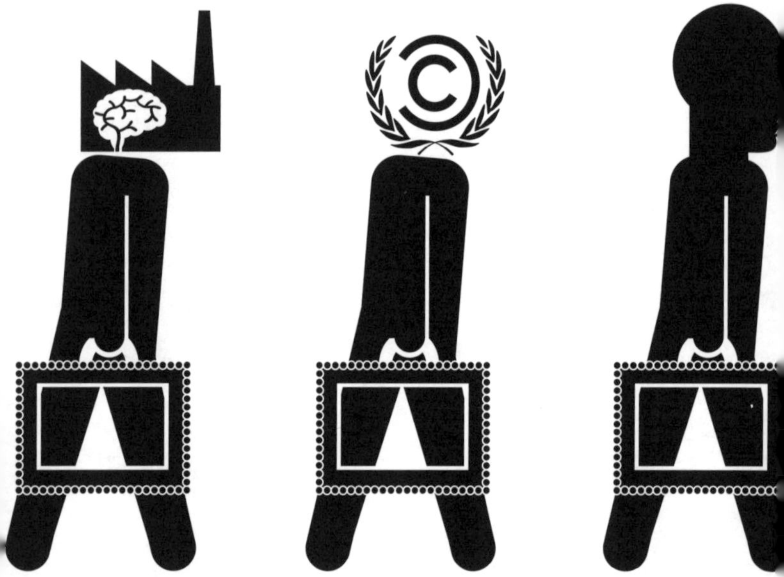

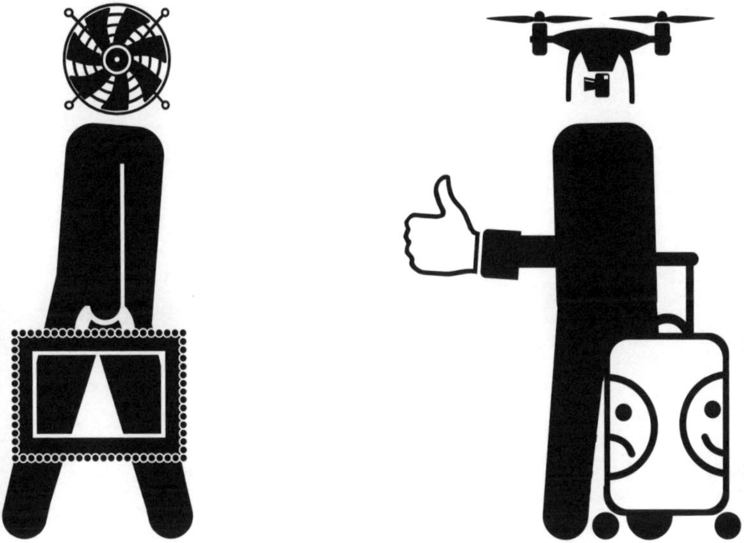

Deserting from the Culture Wars

Edited by Maria Hlavajova
and Sven Lütticken

BAK, basis voor actuele kunst, Utrecht
The MIT Press, Cambridge, MA, and London, England

Table of Contents

Foreword

Maria Hlavajova

This publication brings together artists and other cultural practitioners to intervene in the contemporary condition shaped by the culture wars. The culture wars have been omnipresent for decades, but in the twenty-first century they have assumed a renewed prominence and a polarizing efficacy as a conduit for the gradual normalization of an emerging far-right authoritarian world order. As a significant portion of the globe slides into reaction, battles around civil rights, social and ecological justice, health equity, racial hierarchies, gender identities, and, to be sure, *truth* flood public discourse with a toxic brew of bewildering language, maximalist slogans, manipulative rhetoric, inflammatory imagery, conspiracy theories, and militarized posturing.

This is the "symbolic" artillery deployed in the culture wars. Yet, as I write, the indisputably actual ammunition of rubber bullets, tear gas, riot shields, and batons are being unleashed against protesters taking to the streets in the aftermath of the brutal killing of George Floyd and the many, too many, before him. In Washington, DC, the army of law and order, steel-clad soldiers among them, clear the path for a certain president to walk from one picture-perfect spot, in front of a national flag, to another, in front of a church.[1] Such a politically orchestrated photo op stunt is a quintessential culture wars trope, here overlaid with the intimidating sounds of military helicopters; itself both a tactical response to on-the-ground events and a textbook prop of sickening theatrical swagger. Here too, the culture war dynamic gives the vocabulary of "domination" and "overwhelming force," drawn from the language of counterinsurgency, a performative hold on reality. This footage captures the global imagination so forcefully not just for its blatant cruelty, but also because it issues from a nation that, under the aegis of "democracy" and self-usurped global leadership, has been selling white supremacy as universal freedom. But countless similar scenes go unnoticed elsewhere in the world, as we are forced to brace for the next culture wars skirmish to violently spill out from the online space into the streets. Or into an LGBTQ+ club anywhere in the world. Or onto an island populated with kids in a summer camp. Or under a spray of bleach. Or by exhaustion from crossing vast lands to reach home in an unemployed misery. Or at a grocery store where a disgruntled shopper refuses to wear a facemask to protect others, and thus themself, from the coronavirus. In these conflagrations, the culture wars seamlessly entwine with "other" wars: class wars, civil wars, economic wars, and the active military hostilities. To be sure, culture is not some abstract and distant terrain. Rather, it is the ideological turf for all combat, and thus, to put it simply, where wars are won and lost.

Tumultuous and violent events unfold, accelerated by social media culture warriors, in rapid succession at extreme speed. Undergirded by confusing and fast-changing narratives across several simultaneous fronts, the culture wars seem administered as an anesthetic that disorients, bewilders, and consequently exhausts. The numerous, coterminous, accelerated, multidirectional affronts seem to cross the limits of what one can even process, gaining advantage by pushing those facing the onslaught into a constant reactive mode. How can we *organize differently* and circumvent these totalitarian decoys—*deserting the culture wars*, in other words—and move toward a way of *being together otherwise*?[2]

Within these circumstances, writer and curator Sven Lütticken has conceptualized the project *Deserting from the Culture Wars* (2019–2020) as part of a long-term research, discourse, exhibition, education, and publishing itinerary at BAK, basis voor actuele kunst, titled

Propositions for Non-Fascist Living (2017–ongoing).[3] Lütticken conceives of *tactical desertion* as a way to "actively evade" the ever-more polarized ideological-cultural combat waged in a theater of war demarcated by the far-right through aggressive hypersensitivity, injured entitlement, angry rants, and memes about Cultural Marxism, immigration, climate change, and feminism. Neither a submission to nor an escape from these offensives, the notion of desertion builds upon the genealogy of flight and exodus as artistic and political practices. In sync with artist and political activist Jean-Jacques Lebel's appeal "to desert, but positively"[4]—seeking to circumvent the strictures of the state apparatus and engage in instituent practices instead—Lütticken asks amid the conundrum of today's culture wars: What possibilities would be opened by a refusal to play these war games, and commit desertion—not as a withdrawal into a realm of apolitical privacy, but as a pursuit of different strategies, tactics, and coalitions?

In order to collectively deliberate and publically practice such possibilities, BAK and Lütticken co-convened the weeklong gathering *Propositions #9: Deserting from the Culture Wars* with a number of artists, theorists, and activists.[5] It took a hybrid form of trainings, lectures, and panel discussions and sought not merely to theorize the culture wars at present, but rather to imagine and enact the strategies of desertion as a concrete practice of worldmaking. Nested within yet another project, *Trainings for the Not-Yet* (2019–2020), conceptualized as "an exhibition as a series of trainings for a future of being together otherwise" by artist Jeanne van Heeswijk, *Propositions #9: Deserting from the Culture Wars* borrowed from it the technique of collective "trainings."[6]

For this publication, the gathering functioned as a public editorial assembly of sorts. It unraveled in real time as a

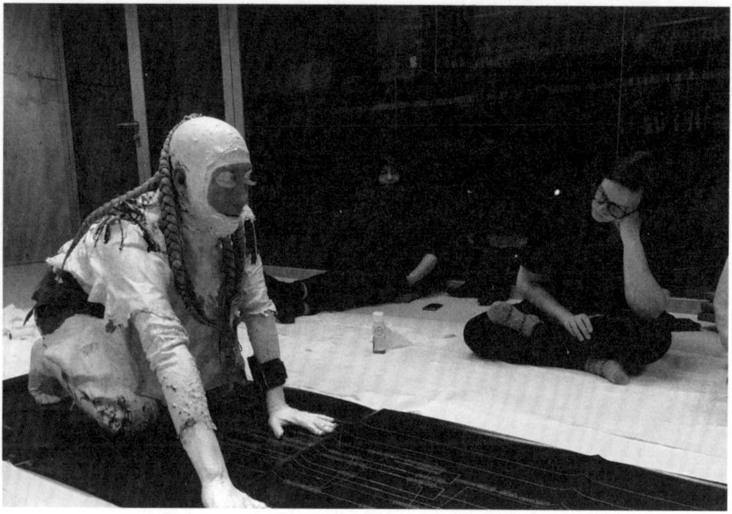

Reprocommunal Training Camp with Transformella Malor in the framework of *Propositions #9: Deserting from the Culture Wars*, BAK, basis voor actuele kunst, Utrecht, 13 November 2019, photo: Sven Lütticken

set of tentative, yet tactile and concrete responses to the quandary of how to conceive of culture as a space of action that is emancipatory, embodied, intersubjective, and driven by demands for social and ecological justice. Here we can see culture as a collective performance and a method of mutual, anticipatory learning that marks a space for the enactment of possibilities radically different from those implied by the hard right's conception of the field. Issuing from this process, this volume brings together texts that mobilize resistance and imagination, and propose ways to embody a non-fascist life. These are the political and ethical commitments that drive BAK as a base for thinking and imagining—and intervening by living these alternative imaginings *as if they were possible*.

In these times, the aesthetico-political apothegm that has shaped BAK's practice over the last twenty-odd

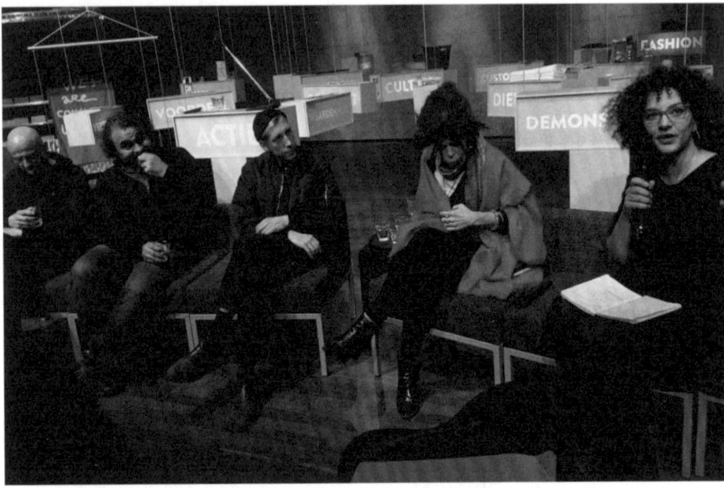

Panel "Working in Groups, Acting in Networks" during *Propositions #9: Deserting from the Culture Wars*, BAK, basis voor actuele kunst, Utrecht, 15 November 2019, photo: Sven Lütticken

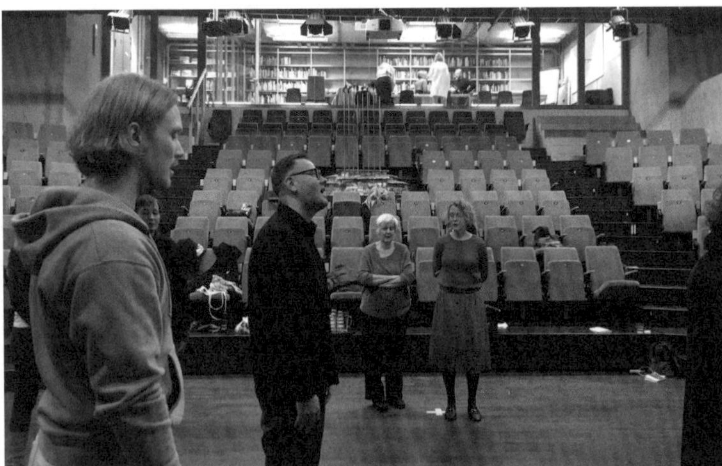

"The Plague" Training with Rose Hammer in the framework of *Propositions #9: Deserting from the Culture Wars*, BAK, basis voor actuele kunst, Utrecht, 14 November 2019, photo: Sven Lütticken

years—*instituting otherwise*—seems to connect more clearly than ever to the dissident knowledges of the underground school of politics I came of age within. In the former European East—but also across various other totalitarian "pasts"—we have seen similar strategies of disengaging with powers that be by "speaking past them" and through affirmative disengagement that meant neither resignation nor retreat but a way of rehearsing that which was yet to come.[7] It was a "training" of sorts, in creating and sustaining "parallel structures" for alternative art and culture.[8] Back then, I could not have imagined how useful this knowledge would prove in the coming century to fight for the possibility of a livable life in common.

I would like to thank all the contributors to this publication for their in-depth analyses and propositions for how to organize ourselves in the face of today's cultural wars: Bini Adamczak, Kader Attia, Rose Hammer, Tom Holert, Geert Lovink, Sven Lütticken, Diana McCarty, Dan McQuillan, Johannes Paul Raether, Natascha Sadr Haghighian, Esmee Schoutens, Andreas Siekmann, and Jonas Staal. Equally, I want to thank all those who took part in the assembly *Propositions #9: Deserting from the Culture Wars*. Most notably, I thank artist Jeanne van Heeswijk from whom we have learned to embrace the notion of training in preparation for the yet to come. Crucially, I owe my appreciation and admiration to Sven Lütticken, who not only convened such a large collective conversation around the subject at hand, but who has always shared his unending reservoir of knowledge and imagination with BAK in comradely solidarity. I thank Wietske Maas, associate editor and Irene Calabuch Mirón, managing editor of this publication for their extraordinary and moving commitment to our shared work. My utmost gratitude goes to my colleagues at BAK, without whom none of what we humbly try to achieve would be imaginable. Last but not least, I thank the book's co-publisher The MIT Press, and Victoria Hindley in particular.

1 "'When fascism comes to America, it will be wrapped in the flag and carrying a cross,' goes an oft-quoted line of uncertain origin." See David Smith, "'Words of a dictator': Trump's threat to deploy military raises spectre of fascism," *The Guardian*, June 2020, https://www.theguardian.com/us-news/2020/jun/02/donald-trump-george-floyd-protests-military-threat.

2 The notion of "instituting otherwise" has been shaping the institutional practice of BAK from its very inception in 2000. Here, "instituting otherwise" is a continuous process and a method of engaging the urgencies of the present *alongside* and *with* the diverse, multi-talented, and poly-vocal constituencies of BAK. At the same time, "instituting otherwise" is a systematic move away from (art) institutions as they persist, specifically in the West and in ways redolent of the colonial era, as custodians of power geared at anesthetization and thus depoliticization and normalization of social, political, ecological, and economic injustices in the world.

3 BAK's long-term research series *Propositions for Non-Fascist Living* (2017–ongoing) explores in, with, and through art the modes of imagining and practicing life—and thus modeling a world—decidedly void of fascisms.

4 Jean-Jacques Lebel, "Dés-ir/Dés-ordre," *À pied, à cheval et en Spoutnik: Quelques écrits 1961–2009* (1977; repr., Paris: Beaux-arts de Paris, 2009), p. 62. Translation by Sven Lütticken. The text was originally published in the catalog Paris-New York, Centre Georges Pompidou, Paris, 1977.

5 Taking place within the BAK series *Propositions for Non-Fascist Living* (2017–ongoing) as its ninth sequence, the assembly occurred from 13–17 November 2019. Participants included: Bini Adamczak, Kader Attia, Maria Hlavajova, Tom Holert, Patricia Kaersenhout, Charl Landvreugd, Sven Lütticken, Diana McCarty, Dan McQuillan, Dina Mohamed, Johannes Paul Raether, Rose Hammer (Stacey E. Devoe, Dora Garcia, Nora Joung, Per-Oskar Leu, and Niels Munk Plum), Natascha Sadr Haghighian, Jonas Staal, Terra Critica (Birgit M. Kaiser and Kathrin Thiele), and Transformella Malor. The complete documentation is available on BAK's online archive.

6 See Maria Hlavajova, "Trainings for the Not-Yet. Introduction," Guidebook *Trainings for the Not-Yet*, 14 September 2019–12 January 2020, BAK, basis voor actuele kunst, Utrecht, pp. 3–7.

7 Tony Judt, *Postwar: A History of Europe Since 1945* (New York: Penguin, 2005), p. 567.

8 See Václav Benda, "The Parallel '*Polis*,'" in *Civic Freedom in Central Europe: Voices from Czechoslovakia*, H. Gordon Skilling and Paul Wilson, eds. (London: Macmillan, 1991), pp. 35–41.

In the following texts please note that, wherever authors have specified their choices of vocabulary and style, this has been retained by the editors.

Performing Culture Otherwise

Sven Lütticken

Père Ubu: Men of Poland, charge!
The Polish Army: I think he means retreat.
Père Ubu: The victory is ours!
The Polish Army: I think he means defeat.[1]

There is the fascism in all of us and there is the fascism coming at us. Interrogating one's inner fascist is one thing; being confronted with outer fascists (even if they stay in the closet and take exception at being identified as fascists) is another.[2] The latter stage a constant stream of "cultural emergencies" that infiltrate the psyche via social media. There is always a petition to sign or something to retweet. And no doubt: there is cause for action when, for instance, a eugenicist twerp is appointed as advisor to Boris Johnson's UK government, or when a far-right figure like Piotr Bernatowicz gets appointed director of the Ujazdowski Castle Center for Contemporary Art (CCA) in Warsaw. If contemporary artists affiliated with prominent and once-respectable galleries use alt-right tropes and troll tactics, that, too, should be cause for concern.[3]

It is often "the left" that is accused of having started the culture wars through its desire to censor, to stifle free speech, or to impose its radical agenda on an unwilling public. This right-wing reframing of emancipatory projects may be the fundamental, inaugural moment of the culture wars. To be sure, "progressives" have frequently been ready to play the part of the bogeyman—of "social justice warriors," as the right-wing lingo has it. The challenges posed to hegemonic identities fueled the rise of new identitarianisms and created markets of grievance, while overreacting to something on Twitter became a certain liberal commentariat's raison d'être (I'm looking at you, *The Guardian*). This is all too patently true, but none of it justifies potted histories, false equivalences, or victim blaming.

Culture wars always have the potential to turn violent. They can become a matter of life and death, as physical violence and acts of murder and terrorism are legitimized—and sometimes triggered—by alt-right culture warriors, from Anders Breivik in Norway to racist shooting sprees in mosques or shisha bars to violence against LGBTQ+ people in Bolsonaro's Brazil.[4] The 2020 resurgence of Black Lives Matter protests after the murder of George Floyd by the Minneapolis police—which Trump, in line with conspiracy theories about "Cultural Marxists" being behind everything that supposedly went wrong in US-American culture, quickly blamed on "Antifa" or "anarchists"—showed precisely that the culture wars are ultimately about the right to breathe. The culture wars shape, break, and end lives. The sense of urgency and constant alarm is all too understandable. Nonetheless, there is the danger of slipping into a purely reactive mode, of becoming a twitching bundle of Pavlovian reflexes. A key countercultural slogan of the Vietnam era was "Suppose they gave a war and no one came" (popular in Germany as *Stell dir vor, es ist Krieg, und keiner geht hin*). How about not joining—or extracting ourselves from—*this* war as it is being waged on terms set by the right?

1. Two and More Cultures

If culture is a battleground, it is worth examining which conception of culture is operative in the waging of culture wars. In the 1980s and 1990s, the United States in particular became the site of "culture wars" —a term canonized by James Davison Hunter in 1991—between opposing forces.[5] Right-wing cultural activism gained momentum throughout the decade: in a 1989 column, Pat Buchanan called for "a cultural revolution in the 90s" that was to be "as sweeping" as the "political revolution in the 80s."[6] There are clear continuities between the culture wars of the late 1980s/early 1990s and those of today. Milo

Yiannopoulos called Trump "the first truly cultural candidate for president since [Pat] Buchanan."[7] Of course, the differences are no less significant: instead of culture wars waged by old men such as Buchanan and Jesse Helms, we have armies of trolls—from *Breitbart* to 4chan to the *Daily Stormer*—who have created an ironic online fascism that goes by the name "alt-right."

The political revolution of the 1980s mentioned by Buchanan was of course that of Reagan, which is to say: the neoliberal rollback of progressive policies from the 1960s and 1970s. Similarly, Buchanan's cultural revolution would of course be a reactionary counterpoint to the cultural revolution of the late 1960s and early 1970s. For Buchanan, as for contemporary culture warriors such as Steve Bannon, this was the original sin, the fall from grace that needed to be undone. The far right identifies this historical moment with the triumph of so-called Cultural Marxism—a notion that began to be used in the early 1990s in the US by the right-wing movement founded and led by Lyndon Larouche.[8] Originating with the Reagan/Bush era culture wars with their skirmishes over political correctness, Cultural Marxism largely came to function as a byword for the challenging of racial hierarchies and traditional gender identities. As a number of observers have noted, Cultural Marxism has overtones of the Nazi expression *Kulturbolschewismus* (Cultural Bolshevism)—and while György Lukács and Antonio Gramsci feature in many genealogies of Cultural Marxism, the Frankfurt School takes center stage because many of its key members spent time in the US (and it started as a US-based and US-centric "theory"), and because of its suitability as anti-Semitic bogeyman.[9]

If Marxism essentially gets reduced to a Jewish conspiracy to destroy white Christian US-American superiority, what about the qualifier "cultural"? The notion of culture at play here is an odd combination of conservative essentialism and cod-Marxist superstructuralism. Raymond Williams and Terry Eagleton, among others, have traced how, beginning from around 1800, the notion of *Kultur* came to function in the context of a Romantic critique of industrial capitalism and of universal Enlightenment notions of civilization. Enlightenment philosopher Johann Gottfried Herder had already argued for the existence of a plurality of cultures, and later anthropologists and ethnographers would seek to arrive at an understanding of them all, even while establishing hierarchies among them.[10] The antagonists of so-called Cultural Marxism take it as a given that US-American culture would under "normal circumstances" reflect the values they ascribe to the (white) population—as is evident, for instance, in Bannon's propaganda films.[11] This is characteristic of conservative conceptions of culture as the reflection of an organic populace's values.

However, in their analysis of the changes that have taken place since the 1960s, the critics of Cultural Marxism graft a schematic superstructuralism onto this organicism. "Culture" comes to stand for the media and academia, spheres infiltrated by evildoers who corrupt and indoctrinate the young and feeble-minded. There is no end to the litanies about "the liberal media" or *Lügenpresse* (lying press), churning out "fake news" in the service of "liberal elites." Such discourse is like a warped, conspiracist reflection of Marx's conceptualization of culture as a superstructure constituted by "the legal, political, religious, artistic or philosophic—in short, ideological forms in which men become conscious of [conflict in the economic base] and fight it out."[12]

This hybrid conception of culture that underlies the right-wing culture wars thus combines a conservative collectivism (culture *should* organically reflect the values of the white, Christian majority) with a cod-Marxist/Gramscian superstructuralism (the ideological *Überbau* has been taken over by the enemy, and hegemony needs to be reconquered). To be sure, the infiltration of the superstructure is considered to have its repercussions on the very composition of the people—after all, the sinister elites are said to have actively pursued a project of "population exchange" and "white genocide" by welcoming (Muslim) immigrants. The post-9/11 success of Samuel Huntington's "clash of civilizations" narrative has had a profound impact on the culture wars.[13]

There is a third element in the right's conception of culture: individualism, or a cult of sovereign individuality. The main contemporary ideologist of individual sovereignty is perhaps Jordan B. Peterson, the Canadian academic crusader against woke "snowflake" culture in the university, who has compared gender theory to Maoism, claiming that they are essentially "the same ideology."[14] Peterson identifies the enemy as "postmodern neo-Marxism" (this being a slightly more academically respectable shibboleth), though some of his videos get reposted with "Cultural Marxism" in the title.[15] Claiming that the current culture war is of a cabal of Marxist postmodernists attacking the "self-evident" truths of the US Declaration of Independence, Peterson provides a theoretical basis for a culture in which "free speech" and the right to voice one's opinion becomes the quintessential white male right.[16] If many on the far right invoke reactionary traditions, Peterson—a seemingly more moderate figure—extolls the Enlightenment in order to shore up a certain notion of entitled white male subjectivity. In this, Peterson is arguably a better "reader" of modernity than Jürgen Habermas, whose liberal paeans to democratic deliberation and public debate minimize their founding exclusions.

Taking aim at Habermas, Achille Mbembe has noted that "late-modern political criticism has unfortunately privileged normative theories of democracy and has made the concept of reason one of the most important elements of both the project of modernity and of the topos of sovereignty."[17] Here, of course, the focus is on political and territorial sovereignty, but the sovereignty of the body politic is ultimately grounded in the individuals who compose the *Volk* or the *demos*. For Habermasian conceptions of democracy, "the ultimate expression of sovereignty is the production of general norms by a body (the *demos*) made up of free and equal men and women. These men and women are posited as full subjects capable of self-understanding, self-consciousness, and self-representation."[18] What Habermas ignores is that the *demos* was always exclusionary and that any definition of the *demos* in terms of free men (and later also women) was grounded in the necropolitical production of bare life, at home and especially in the colonies. Habermas's Enlightenment-fetishist conception of democracy is blind when it comes to its own complicity with a regime that has always racialized rationality. In Denise Ferreira da Silva's terminology, the "transparent I" of the supposedly universal rational subject has as its counterpart a (racialized, gendered) "affectable I" deemed incapable of (self-)control.[19] This is precisely how certain supposedly leftist universalists today can end up strengthening right-wing narratives: by doggedly refusing to address universalism's compromised nature.

In today's culture wars, reactionaries reassert the right of white men to be sovereign subjects at the cost of others, and of the white population to assert its sovereignty collectively. While the proselytizers of individual sovereignty may not be the same people who harp on about the organic collectivity of the people (or the white race), these are ultimately two sides of social Darwinism. Rather than a single ideology, contemporary neofascism is "a tangled skein of wayward visions."[20] In this assemblage of tendencies and movements, Peterson's emphasis on strong male sovereign individuality resonates. It is fuel for right-wing culture warriors who may also hold positions that go far beyond what Peterson himself is willing to endorse. (When it comes to race, Peterson is more careful than when it comes to gender, though he knows how to use a dog whistle.)

As analyzed by scholars such as Robert O. Paxton, fascist speech was never about ideological consistency, but about agency and effect. Fascist speech acts are literally fighting words, designed to anticipate and, depending on the circumstances, instigate violence. In the 1920s to 1940s, this operation was largely executed through propaganda by media professionals. If modern culture was a superstructure maintained by a cadre of experts, culture today has expanded to the point of bursting. It is a continuous performance by whoever wants to get in on the act. There may be organizers, powerful companies, and think tanks directing operations, but if you are posting angry rants about immigrants, gender, or climate change online, you are a freelancer in the culture wars—even if you just get the latest PragerU videos in your feed.

Though the right often upholds a lofty and elitist ideal of culture in theory, it has embraced a more profane version that is lived and performed in daily practice. Their initiatives foster a troll subjectivity marked by aggressive hypersensitivity, injured entitlement, and confidence in their status as sovereign. Far from limiting the performance of culture to one-sided speech acts, to the abstract "right to say something," an emancipatory understanding of culture needs to conceive of it as embodied and intersubjective—as a relational performance in which, as per Karen Barad,

Ron Paul @RonPaul · 3 min

Are you stunned by what has become of American culture? Well, it's not an accident. You've probably heard of "Cultural Marxism," but do you know what it means? ... More here: facebook.com/ronpaul/photos...

Oversett tweet

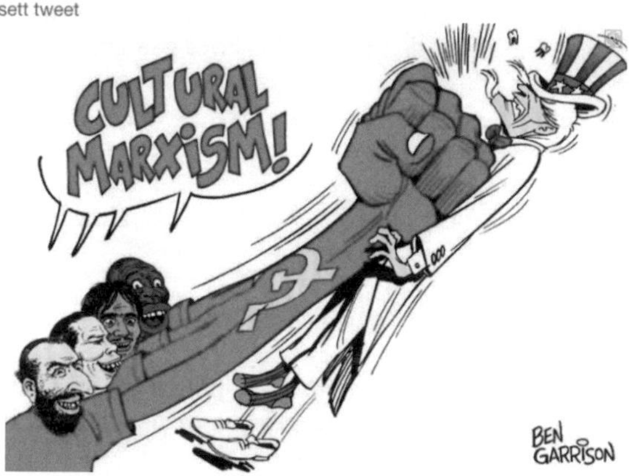

3 14 26

Ron Paul, Twitter post,
7 February 2018 (deleted)

the relations do not follow from the relata, but the other way around.[21]

2. Avant-Garde, Desertion, Fugitivity

Since the early 1970s, capitalism has been in a long slump. For all the creative disruptions of Silicon Valley-led global capitalism since 1989, the neoliberal era has been structured by stagnation. It is a "long crisis," in the words of Joshua Clover, one marked by a decline in production and an ongoing financialization of the economy.[22] The key year was 1973, with its oil crisis, the collapse of Bretton Woods, the inauguration of the Chicago Options Exchange, and the introduction of the Black-Scholes model.[23] The subsequent decades have seen massive wealth redistribution to the top as a substitute for growth, rising income and wealth disparities, indebtedness, and surplus populations. The long crisis, which has since become an accelerating catastrophe, is our contemporary condition. As Wolfgang Streeck sketches the future foreseeable in this framework:

> [E]ver new ways will be sought to exploit nature, extend and intensify working time, and encourage what the jargon calls creative finance, in a desperate effort to keep profits up and capital accumulation going. The scenario of "stagnation with a chance of bubbles" may most plausibly be imagined as a battle of all against all, punctured by occasional panics and with the playing of endgames becoming a popular pastime.[24]

This war can take on the form of what Clover, in turn, calls "surplus rebellions."[25] In contrast to the industrial era with its organized labor movement and strikes, the age of precarity and surplus labor sees an increase in riots. These riots are often racialized, from the US-American "race riots" of the 1960s to this year's George Floyd/Black Lives Matter uprising (where the distinction between riots and peaceful protests seemed irrelevant in the eyes of Trump and his supporters).

The long crisis has not only tended to undermine the strike (though strikes, of course, continue to be organized), it has had consequences for organizing more broadly. Today's theoretical nostalgia for the Party is a symptom of its decline, and the very idea of a revolutionary avant-garde is likewise not unaffected. Arriving at the tail end of the West's postwar period of prosperity, May '68—the right-wing culture warriors' favorite bogeyman—was a highly ambiguous event in which various "May '68s" coexisted and intermingled, from the Maoist to the anarcho-libertarian.[26] Many interpreted May '68 through the classicizing lens of Marxist-Leninist or Maoist theory, and indeed, the industrial strikes that accompanied the student protests seemed to suggest that the industrial working class could still (help) constitute a revolutionary subject. In France, Italy, Germany, and elsewhere, groups such as Maoists and Operaists moved into the factories to try to help radicalize and organize the workers. At least for the Operaists and their German allies, the focus was on the unskilled "mass worker."[27]

If, during the 1920s, Lenin argued that the political revolution of the Soviet Union needed to be complemented and completed by a cultural revolution, the long event of May '68 was a cultural revolution looking for a political revolution. May '68-affiliated theorists from Herbert Marcuse to Hans-Jürgen Krahl noted the rising importance of scientific, intellectual, and cultural labor, which meant the superstructure was now increasingly integrated with the base, and a growing cognitariat was part of the new labor force.[28] Marcuse argued that in contemporary capitalism, the working class had been extended to:

> include (as sources of surplus value and therefore as "productive labor") a very large part of the "middle classes": white collar workers, salaried employees, technicians, scientists, specialists of all sorts, even in the mere "service industries," publicity, etc. This means the extension of exploitation as an objective condition (though to very different degrees of intensity) among an increasingly large part of the population.[29]

Culture could no longer be conceived of as a series of symbolic skirmishes in which the *real* conflict was fought out in ideological terms; it was now part of the real conflict, and was perhaps its vanguard. In the long crisis, culture became a crucial site of value extraction and wealth redistribution from bottom to top.[30] Its workers are structurally pitted against each other as creative entrepreneurial subjects. To invoke Bini Adamczak: capitalist value connects people together by first separating and dividing them.[31] Within the parameters of neoliberal capitalism, the denizens of this new culture class were in many ways agents of transformation; in the long wake of 1968, and in conjunction with autonomist, feminist, queer, and decolonial groups and networks, they effected a "long cultural revolution" that would in turn trigger a backlash. Welcome to the culture wars, in which the emancipatory agenda of the late-1960s cultural revolution—with its critique of privilege, hierarchies, and bourgeois conventions—is turned into a sinister conspiracy that serves as a perfect foil for the defenders of hierarchy, privilege, and practically neo-feudal forms of sovereignty over subaltern surplus populations.

By the mid-1970s, it was becoming clear that the moment for a "classical" revolutionary break with capitalism had truly passed, and that culture was trailblazing a new phase of capitalism rather than inaugurating the socialist spring.

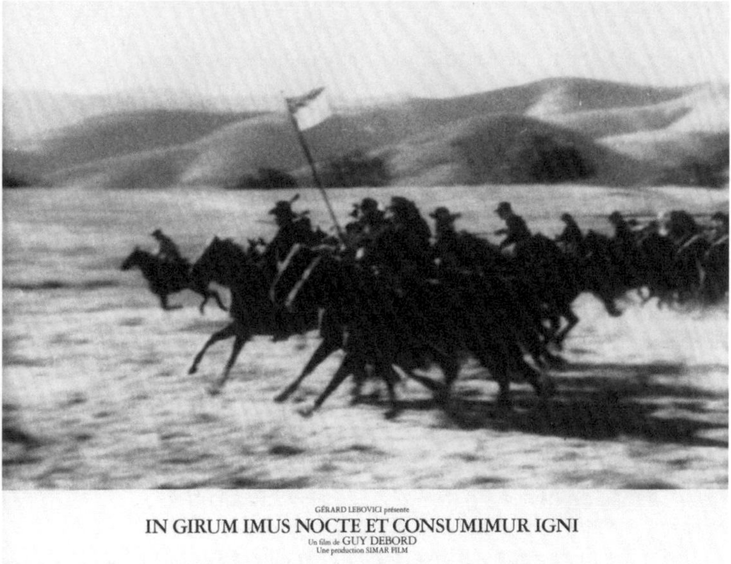

Guy Debord, *In girum imus nocte et consumimur igni* (We Spin Around the Night Consumed by the Fire), 1981, lobby card, source: artprecium

This raised profound questions about the concept of the avant-garde, both politically and aesthetically. It was in the context of radical politics after the French Revolution that the military concept of the vanguard had come to be applied to art's role in society. In 1825, a follower of Saint-Simon wrote a dialogue positing that artists would serve as the avant-garde of the new society that was emerging.[32] Much ink has since been spilled on the subsequent fractious relations between the artistic avant-garde and the political avant-garde, as in the early Soviet Union or in the West during the 1920s and 1930s.

In the postwar era, Situationist International sought to be more than a "mere" artistic avant-garde, and in its attempt to become a "proper" political avant-garde it expelled most of its artists. Its de facto leader, Guy Debord, conceived of May '68 as an anti-Leninist, council-communist revolution. Debord's work is rife with military tropes and imagery. He read and published Carl von Clausewitz, detourned footage from *The Charge of the Light Brigade* (1936) to illustrate Situationist campaigns in his film *In girum imus nocte et consumimur igni* (We Spin Around the Night Consumed by the Fire, 1978), and spent much time on developing and marketing his *Game of War*.[33] That Debord's military fetish seems to have become more prominent in the 1970s, when he increasingly looked like a general without troops, is suggestive. At the same time, a mutation or inversion of the avant-garde's military imaginary occurred in other milieus.

A case in point is a 1977 text by Jean-Jacques Lebel—another May '68 veteran—who had largely withdrawn from the institutional art world. In an essay written for the catalog of an early Centre Pompidou exhibition, Lebel reflected on the museum as a spearhead of "urban renewal" (or gentrification) as being a betrayal of the '68 promise of lived creativity in favor of dead art, as well as on the rise of Autonomia and the *Indiani Metropolitani* in Italy. In response to this constellation of topics, he closes with a "scenario for a happening" titled "Strategy for Victory" that proposes:

> To abandon that which is confining, destructive or negatively repetitive.
> To open up to that which creates and increases autonomy.
> To put one's energies and desires into a social position for the production and exchange of subversive and non-suicidal intensities.
> To desert, but positively.[34]

The text is informed both by Gilles Deleuze and Félix Guattari, to whom Lebel was close, and by the rise of post-Operaist Autonomism (and, of course, closely following developments in Italy, where the Operaist focus on workers' autonomy had given way to a more general focus on autonomist self-organization that was no longer tied to the fading promise of proletarian revolution).[35] The same phenomenon can be seen elsewhere; in Germany, where the post-'68 Sponti movement drew inspiration from Italian Operaismo and Autonomia, attempts at organization on the factory floor gave way to a focus on *autonome Lebensformen* (autonomous forms of life), centered around squats and small self-organized initiatives and companies. Some argued that it hardly amounted to a serious strategy to idealize a certain alternative left-wing scene as the nucleus of the socialism to come.[36]

In this context, Deleuze and Guattari-inspired notions of flight, exodus, and desertion came to feature heavily in artistic and activist discourse of the period. Deleuze and Guattari themselves quoted George Jackson in *Anti-Oedipus: Capitalism and Schizophrenia* (1977): "I may take flight, but all the while I am fleeing, I will be looking for a weapon."[37] This became a reference for the elaboration of the concept of lines of flight in *A Thousand Plateaus* (1987), taken up again by more recent autonomist theorists: "The combination of flight and invention, of the desertion from the state apparatus and the movement of instituting, the invention of an *instituent flight* is the specific quality of the war machine."[38] Meanwhile, like Lebel in the 1970s, the Invisible Committee translates this into the more overtly (anti-)military register of "desertion," emphasizing "the decision to desert, to desert the ranks, to organize, to undertake a secession, be it imperceptibly, but in any case, *now.*"[39]

Recently, philosopher Peter Osborne has problematized the belief "that freedom does appear directly politically in a movement," which he associates with (post-)Operaismo and Autonomia, and "that it can do so only through *withdrawal* ('exodus') from the existing capitalistic form of the social."[40] Osborne avers that:

> in an ironic mimesis of the autonomous work of art, such *autonomy from*—or separation from—prevailing forms of social practice makes the exercise of any such positive freedom *impotent*; impotence famously being the price of autonomous art's criticality. Political autonomy, in the Autonomia tradition, is thus not so much the negation of the autonomy of the artwork as its ironic political mimesis.[41]

However, this diagnosis is perhaps more applicable to the political lineage that runs from the late-1960s American New Communalist movement (of which Stewart Brand's *Whole Earth Catalog* was an exponent), to contemporary cyberlibertarians/cyberfascists from Nick Land to Peter Thiel. While the New Communalists revived the frontier myth and fled to the land, cultural theorist Ana Teixeira Pinto notes that for the latter, the right to exit, to opt out, is "the only meaningful right." This kind of exiting, she notes, hinges on leaving others behind; it is "the formal version of what is informally known as 'white flight.'"[42] If the lines between this "exitism" and autonomist flight, exodus and desertion can be blurry, a key distinction must nonetheless be made. As architect and activist Stavros Stavrides notes, from an autonomist perspective:

> I am thus very suspicious or reserved about the idea that we can build our own small enclaves of otherness, our small liberated strongholds that

> could protect us from the power of the state. I don't mean that it is not important to build communities of resistance, but rather than framing them as isolated enclaves, we should attempt to see them as a potential network of resistance, collectively representing only a part of the struggle. If you tend to believe that a single community with its commons and its enclosed parameter could be a stronghold of liberated otherness, then you are bound to be defeated.[43]

The popularity of Autonomism in certain parts of the art world is one indication of the increased centrality of organizational matters in art since the 1970s. Aware of their role as freelancing foot soldiers of the capitalist cultural revolution, cultural workers nonetheless sought to perform culture differently—from institutional critique to a proliferation of self-organized spaces and platforms. In one significant recent move, Fred Moten and Stefano Harney have argued that Autonomism has a "debt at a distance to the black radical tradition. In Autonomia, in the militancy of post-workerism, there is no outside, refusal takes place inside and makes its break, its flight, its exodus from the inside."[44] This is at the basis of Harney and Moten's take on undercommoning institutions that are beyond meaningful reform by forming Maroon communities in the university and elsewhere. On the other hand, certain forms of institutional critique or "institutional liberation" still have hope to transform even the most implacable of juggernauts: Tate gave up its BP sponsorship, activists forced William Kanders to resign from the Whitney's board, the Sackler family's patronage is under general attack, and the opening of the "woke" new MoMA in 2020 was accompanied by comments to the effect that a more inclusive and diverse collection is not, in itself, enough, as Jack McGrath writes:

> The prospect of a 21st century WPA may ultimately rescue art institutions from their dependency on banks and billionaires, but in the meantime, it is high time museum boards heed protesters' call and purge themselves of the worst offenders. If not, all the good work of more enlightened curation will be seen, correctly, as so much art-washing—mere instruments to launder the funds and reputations of a globally predatory elite.[45]

During the coronavirus crisis, it soon became evident how museums that avow progressive values operate when push comes to shove. MoMA, that monument of obscene wealth, quickly cancelled contracts with its freelance educators. Museum education departments in the US tend to be more ethnically diverse than others, and the museum thus shoved people from some of the most vulnerable groups into the line of fire.[46] Predictably, after the George Floyd killing, MoMA published a call for "equity and justice" on its home page.

In art, the economic, social, and psychic crisis of Covid-19 quickly established a new normal of a neoliberal attention economy 2.0, with relentless pressure to perform. As institutions closed their venues and gatherings became impossible, social media and video platforms became the privately-owned forums for performing culture. In the Covid-19 version of the attention economy, which relegated many cultural workers to a position of "non-essential" precarity, it became imperative to share personal musings, videos, reading tips, recipes, and doodles. Under such conditions, the paradoxes of prefigurative practice—how to forge ties of solidarity and build autonomy in an economy designed to either prevent or instrumentalize it—only become more vexing and perplexing.

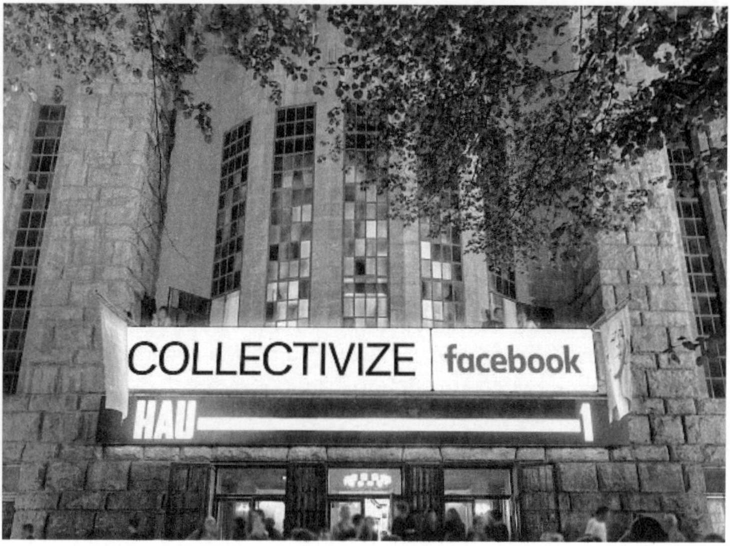

Announcement of Jonas Staal and Jan Fermon's *Collectivize Facebook* pre-trial event at HAU Hebbel am Ufer, Berlin, 2020

Even as Facebook, Zoom, and other platforms were experiencing record traffic, artist Jonas Staal and lawyer Jan Fermon launched their Collectivize Facebook campaign—not with the planned assembly in Berlin, but online, using some of the same platforms that their campaign argues (compellingly) need to be put on a different economic and organizational footing.[47] For museums, as for twenty-first century tech corporations or government agencies, the *Organisationsfrage* (organizational question) is paramount.[48] Deserting positively from the culture wars must mean to exit from forms of sovereign individuality forged through property and competition; to abandon behavioral patterns born from isolation and the fear of social decline; to perform otherwise by relating differently; to transform or undercommon existing institutional structures; to institute otherwise; and to create para-institutions or artist' organizations, collective personae and operational fictions, connections and coalitions.[49]

3. You and What International?

Raymond Williams, one of the progenitors of cultural studies, distinguished between residual, dominant, and emergent social forms:

> By "emergent" I mean, first, that new meanings and values, new practices, new relationships and kinds of relationship are continually being created. But it is exceptionally difficult to distinguish between those which are really elements of some new phase of the dominant culture . . . and those which are substantially alternative or oppositional to it: emergent in the strict sense, rather than merely novel.[50]

As a Marxist, Williams thought of the classic example of the rise of first the bourgeoisie, and then the working class and the new cultural forms they generated, but more broadly, he noted that in any given society, "there is always other social being and consciousness which is neglected and excluded: alternative perceptions of others, in immediate relationships; new perceptions and practices of the material world."[51] Are there ways of intervening actively in processes of emergence—in forming them? After all, for Williams, emergence "depends crucially on finding new forms or adaptations of form."[52] In the culture wars, some on the left look to the 1930s and the Popular Front orchestrated by Moscow; this, after all, was the period of the original culture wars waged by and against fascism.[53] More generally, the decline of organized labor during the long crisis has spawned a neo-Communism in political theory and art, with some positing that what is needed is a return of the Party. But the Party requires comrades. In contrast to the victimhood often claimed by today's identitarians (fascist as well as minoritarian), political theorist Jodi Dean claims that the "term 'comrade' points to a relation, a set of expectations for action. It doesn't name an identity; it highlights the sameness of those who share a politics, a common horizon of political action."[54] While Dean's work may be marked by a refusal to provincialize a certain Bolshevist universalism or acknowledge its factual self-provincialization, her insistence on the need to relate otherwise than in accordance with the imperatives of neoliberalism is valid and valuable—particularly her insistence that "comrade names a relation characterized by sameness, equality, and solidarity. For communists, this sameness, equality, and solidarity is utopian, cutting through the determinations of capitalist society."[55] In this context of long crisis becoming accelerating catastrophe, the specter of the international raises its head again. As Staal put it:

> [W]hile the Comintern was brutally weaponized, the lack of a Transnationale today shows its disastrous consequences: authoritarian-capitalist states pursuing aggressive foreign policies dominate transnational trade and military agreements, and subsidize corporate actors that disproportionately influence our political and economic life. This leads to terrifying situations in which the Rojavans, who bravely fought and sacrificed to protect their multiethnic and multireligious region in North Syria against the Islamic State while establishing their own feminist democracy in the process, are forced to ask support from the Trump regime as the Erdoğan dictatorship threatens with their massacre. As Kurdish Women's Movement activist and thinker Dilar Dirik argued,

> that would be the moment to call upon a "Left Air Brigade"—but in the post-Comintern world, there is no such thing.[56]

If we are "lacking a Comintern" in the fight against the fascist transnational, and more broadly against the version of neoliberal capitalist globalization that is neofascism's raison d'être, then what could such an anti-fascist and anti-capitalist International look like? Is any speculation on that point bound to be frivolous, a mere pipe dream by armchair Leninists? If the right is careful to build up sinister enemies like Antifa, then how can one create collective personae that are also functioning organizations with some degree of real agency over the narratives in which they function? Can the machinery of networked surveillance capitalism be used to foster forms of decision making that would actually enable a "Left Air Brigade," as well as a myriad of less spectacular activities? That the questions are tentative and gauche (never mind the possible answers) may be the strongest indication that these are the right questions. Asking and discussing them is one way of giving the specter a degree of reality and agency. Thinking through the International to come as an *unrealistic necessity* can help us take stock of possibilities and impossibilities, necessities to contend with, and chances worth taking.

The matter only becomes more urgent in the context of 2020's retrenchment, as national sovereignty quickly became reestablished through closed borders, and the state of exception made some governments and leaders act like cartoon versions of an Agambenian sovereign, wielding power over life and death. In the US, where people of color were dying disproportionately from Covid-19, the toddler dictator tried to crush Black Lives Matter protests with police violence even while encouraging his

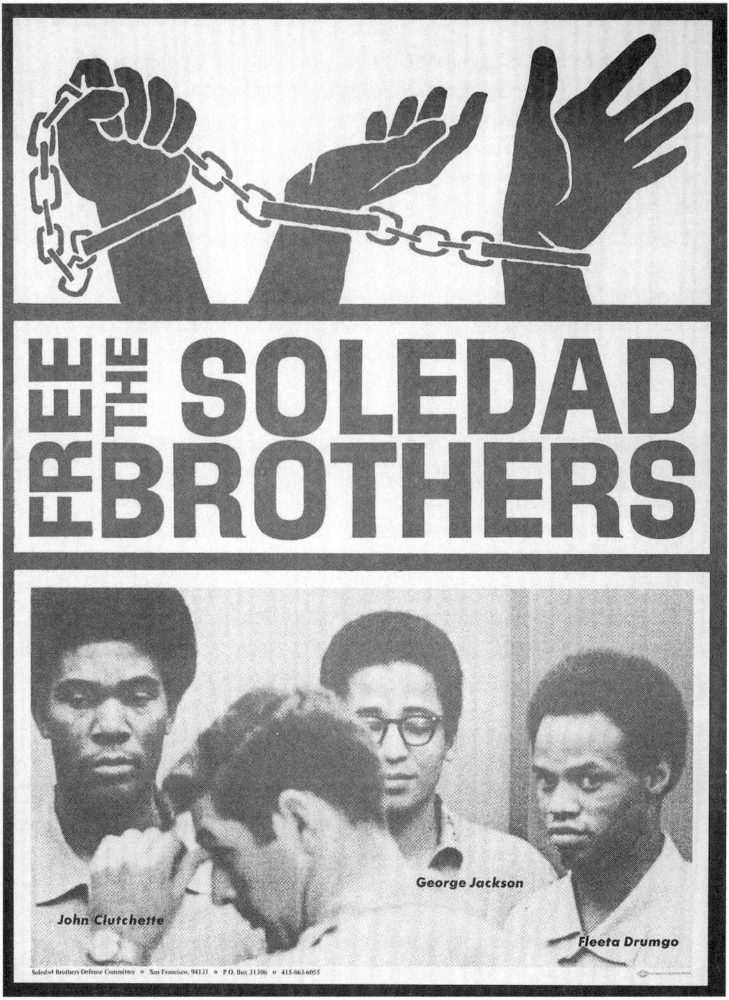

Soledad Brothers Defense Committee, *Free the Soledad Brothers*, 1970, poster, source: pinterest followers to protest against his own government's coronavirus restrictions, using the ideological trope of government overreach. European neofascists have likewise used this opportunity. In Germany, a coalition of far-right Querfront activists brought hordes of angry citizens, alt-right hipsters, conspiracy theorists, and anti-vaxxers together for protests in several cities.[57] A new political movement emerged that was in many ways the coronavirus version of the anti-Muslim and anti-immigrant Pegida; once again, politicians fumbled in their responses. Meanwhile, states such as Russia and China sponsor Covid-19 disinformation campaigns in the EU.[58]

Pronouncements on the waning of capitalist globalization in favor of a restoration of older forms of sovereignty are overhasty. There has always been a conflict-ridden complicity between global capitalism and the nation-state, and many of today's right-wing governments represent de facto takeovers of the state by high finance. The US-American campaign to "reopen" the economy used familiar far-right culture-war tropes ("social distancing is a communist plot!") and was not just supported rhetorically by Trump but also financially and organizationally by the Koch family.[59] As Clover suggests: "We need to stop fucking around with theory and say, without hesitation, that capitalism, with its industrial body and crown of finance, is sovereign; that carbon emissions are the sovereign breathing; that *make work and let buy* must be annihilated; that there is no survival while the sovereign lives."[60]

While the three main historical Internationals were built on alliances between labor movements in—and later the governments of—nation-states, today class composition is a messier affair, and the level of the nation is less privileged than before, if only because the nation-state and its media are the natural habitat of fascism. This is not to relapse into a "small is beautiful" ideology, but to think in terms of alliances and assemblages across scales. Murray Bookchin's confederalism, which became so central to the revolutionary process in Rojava, provides some pointers here: Bookchin posits "a confederal network of municipal assemblies" that can "[reduce] the corporate economy . . . to a truly political economy in which municipalities, interacting with each other economically as well as politically, will resolve their material problems as citizen bodies in open assemblies."[61] Of course, analog and situated, as well as digital and distributed assemblies and councils will run up against massive obstacles as long as there are emergent forms, or forms failing to truly emerge, under the conditions of actually existing neoliberalism and fascism.

With authors such as Bruno Latour, Déborah Danowski, and Eduardo Viveiros de Castro positing that the true conflict of the twenty-first century is not that of class warfare along familiar modern lines, let alone the "race war" fantasized (and enacted) by white supremacists, but that between Humans and "Terrans."[62] The Humans are the heirs to the false universalism of the Enlightenment subject: extractivist sovereigns reducing large swathes of the globe to *terra nullius*, and subjects to objects. The Terrans, meanwhile, are a motley crew. Clearly, while the figure of the Terran is at its root an indigenist one, "Terranship" must be conceived of as an open assemblage rather than in terms of exclusively indigenous membership. Deserting from the culture wars means building the Terrestrial, and this process takes the form of (at times fractious and doomed) patchworks of minorities, concatenated and conflicting organizational forms, and networks of groups.

While the concepts of the comrade and the Terran spring from vastly different imaginaries, properly understood, becoming-Terran must entail becoming-comrade, and vice versa; not becoming-comrade in the sense of a single Party or centrally-led Comintern, but in the sense of assemblies and assemblages bringing together the all-too-human mutants and monsters of actually existing capitalism, in the process of becoming otherwise. Less than a pure constructivist vision, the Terrestrial is something like a Merzbau. The coronavirus crisis having intensied preexisting economic and social tendencies (socialism for the rich, disaster capitalism for the rest), the bricolage is only becoming more precarious. Linking up in conspiracies and cooperatives, in undercommoned bureaucracies and self-organized councils, the Terrans dissemble and assemble, fleeing a contemporaneity that does not take desertion lightly.

1 Père Ubu With Sarah Jane Morris, "Watching the Pigeons," track 10 on *Long Live Père Ubu!*, Cooking Vinyl, COOK CD 497, 2009, compact disc.

2 Michel Foucault theorized the "fascism in all of us" in his preface to the 1984 edition *Anti-Oedipus: Capitalism and Schizophrenia*, by Gilles Deleuze and Félix Guattari, trans. Robert Hurley et al. (1977; repr., London: Continuum, 2004), which is at the basis of BAK's *Propositions for Non-Fascist Living* research series (2017–ongoing).

3 See Ana Teixeira Pinto and Kerstin Stakemeier, "A Brief Glossary of Social Sadism," *Texte zur Kunst*, no. 116 (December 2019), https://www.textezurkunst.de/116/ein-kurzes-glossar-zum-sozialen-sadismus.

4 In her preface to Paul B. Preciado's *Un appartement sur Uranus* (Paris: Grasset, 2019, p. 11), Virginie Despentes notes that as she was writing, the gay Brazilian congressman Jean Wyllys announced that he would be leaving the country, as he feared for his life.

5 James Davison Hunter, *Culture Wars: The Struggle to Define America* (New York: Basic Books, 1991).

6 Quoted in Richard Serra, "Art and Censorship," in *Writings, Interviews* (Chicago: University of Chicago Press, 1994), p. 218. As Brian Wallis noted, "One irony of this struggle over representation is that it is conservative politicians and intellectuals who have most effectively colonized culture as a site of ideological struggle in the 1980s. This is particularly ironic since their claim is generally that culture should be nonideological, free from politics."

Brian Wallis, "Democracy and Cultural Activism," in *Democracy: A Project by Group Material*, ed. Brian Wallis (Seattle: Bay Press, 1990), p. 8.

7 Angela Nagle, *Kill All Normies: Online Culture Wars from Tumblr and 4chan to the Alt-Right and Trump* (Winchester: Zero Books, 2017), p. 54.

8 Martin Jay, "Dialectic of Counter-Enlightenment: The Frankfurt School as Scapegoat of the Lunatic Fringe," *Salmagundi*, no. 168/169 (Fall 2010–Winter 2011), pp. 30–40. I discuss the genealogy of the notion of Cultural Marxism in my essay "Cultural Marxists Like Us," *Afterall*, no. 46 (Autumn/Winter 2018), pp. 67–75, on which I draw here.

9 As one neo-Nazi put it in the description of a YouTube video, with a clarity that is muffled in the more "sophisticated" versions: "The Frankfurt School began in 1923 in Frankfurt, Germany. Its staff was 100% Jewish. Its mission was to destroy White Western Christian culture in order to pave the way for global Marxism," https://www.youtube.com/watch?v=ghx3d1GiAco, accessed 6 July 2017. Under a video of Andrew Breitbart lecturing on Cultural Marxism, a commenter has helpfully added, "He doesn't go into ethnic groups, but you can read between the lines," https://www.youtube.com/watch?v=ZIO40SLwK3A , accessed 7 May 2020. And elsewhere, on the site *Stormfront*: "Talking about the Frankfurt School is ideal for not naming the *Jews as a group* (which often leads to a panicky rejection, a stubborn refusal to listening anymore and even a 'shut up') but naming the *Jew by proper names*. People will make their generalizations by themselves—in the privacy of their own minds," https://www.stormfront.org/forum/t633959-3/.

10 Raymond Williams, *Keywords: A Vocabulary of Culture and Society*. Rev. ed. (New York: Oxford University Press, 1983), pp. 87–93; Terry Eagleton, *The Idea of Culture* (Oxford: Blackwell, 2000), pp. 1–35.

11 In his exhibition *Steve Bannon: A Propaganda Retrospective* (2018) at Het Nieuwe Instituut in Rotterdam, Jonas Staal unpacked key tropes and motifs from Bannon's films, in addition to highlighting his other activities.

12 Karl Marx, preface to *A Contribution to the Critique of Political Economy* (1859; repr., Moscow: Progress Publishers, 1977), https://www.marxists.org/archive/marx/works/1859/critique-pol-economy/preface.htm.

13 In his original 1993 article, Samuel Huntington defines a civilization as "the highest cultural grouping of people and the broadest level of cultural identity people have short of that which distinguishes humans from other species." Samuel P. Huntington, "The Clash of Civilizations?," *Foreign*

Affairs, vol. 72, no. 3 (Summer 1993), p. 24.

14 Channel 4 News, "Jordan Peterson Debate on the Gender Pay Gap, Campus Protests and Postmodernism," 16 January 2018, https://www.youtube.com/watch?v=aMcjxSThD54. Within less than two weeks of its posting, the video had more than seven million clicks.

15 See Jordan B. Peterson, "Postmodern NeoMarxism: Diagnosis and Cure" (lecture, University of Toronto, Toronto, 28 June 2017), https://www.youtube.com/watch?v=s4c-jOdPTN8; Jordan B. Peterson, "Postmodernism and Cultural Marxism," 6 July 2017, https://www.youtube.com/watch?v=wLoG9zBvvLQ.

16 See Jordan B. Peterson, "The Meaning and Reality of Individual Sovreignty" (lecture, Independent Institute, San Francisco, 2 May 2019), https://www.youtube.com/watch?v=JpA5iDpnrbw.

17 Achille Mbembe, "Necropolitics," trans. Libby Meintjes, *Public Culture*, vol. 15, no. 1 (2003), p. 13.

18 Ibid.

19 Denise Ferreira da Silva, *Toward a Global Idea of Race* (Minneapolis: University of Minnesota Press, 2007).

20 Ana Teixeira Pinto, "Capitalism with a Transhuman Face: The Afterlife of Fascism and the Digital Frontier," *Third Text*, vol. 33, no. 3 (2019), p. 320.

21 Karen Barad, *Meeting the Universe Halfway: Quantum Physics and the Entanglement of Matter and Meaning* (Durham: Duke University Press, 2007), pp. 136–137.

22 Joshua Clover, *Riot. Strike. Riot: The New Era of Uprisings* (London: Verso Books, 2016), pp. 129–152.

23 Ibid., pp. 131–132.

24 Wolfgang Streeck, "How Will Capitalism End?," *New Left Review*, no. 87 (May–June 2014), p. 58.

25 Clover, *Riot. Strike. Riot*, pp. 153–174.

26 On the different May '68s, see Alain Badiou, *The Communist Hypothesis*, trans. David Macey and Steve Corcoran (London: Verso Books, 2010), pp. 43–67.

27 See Steve Wright, *Storming Heaven: Class Composition and Struggle in Italian Autonomist Marxism* (London: Pluto Press, 2002), pp. 76–81, 107–108, 176–196. For Germany, see Sebastian Kasper, *Spontis: Eine Geschichte antiautoritärer Linker im roten Jahrzehnt* (Münster: Edition Assemblage,

2019), pp. 33–37, 51–66. The key figure in the German theorization and historiography of the mass worker was Karl-Heinz Roth.

28 See Hans-Jürgen Krahl, "Thesen zum allgemeinen Verhältnis von wissenschaftlicher Intelligenz und proletarischem Klassenbewusstsein," in *Konstitution und Klassenkampf. Zur historischen Dialektik von bürgerlicher Emanzipation und proleratischer Revolution. Schriften, Reden und Entwürfe aus den Jahren 1966–1970* (1969; repr., Frankfurt am Main: Verlag Neue Kritik, 2007), pp. 336–351. On Krahl as an early theorist of the "cognitariat" and the need for new organizational forms, see Franco "Bifo" Berardi, *The Soul at Work: From Alienation to Autonomy*, trans. Francesca Cadel and Guiseppina Mecchia (Los Angeles: Semiotext(e), 2009), p. 66.

29 Herbert Marcuse, "Cultural Revolution," *Towards a Critical Theory of Society: Collected Papers, Vol. 2*, ed. Douglas Kellner (n.d., ca. 1970; repr., London: Routledge, 2001), p. 127.

30 See, for instance, Andrea Fraser, "Le 1%, C'est Moi," *Texte zur Kunst*, no. 83 (September 2011), pp. 114–127; "There's No Place Like Home," *Texte zur Kunst*, no. 83 (September 2011), pp. 144–160.

31 Bini Adamczak, *Beziehungsweise Revolution: 1917, 1968 und kommende* (Berlin: Suhrkamp, 2017), p. 75.

32 The author of the dialogue "L'artiste, le savant et l'industriel" was presumably Olinde Rodrigues. See Matei Calinescu, *Five Faces of Modernity: Modernism, Avant-Garde, Decadence, Kitsch, Postmodernism* (Durham: Duke University Press, 1987), pp. 102–105.

33 A small edition of the Guy Debord's *Game of War* board game was produced in 1977, in time for it to be featured in *In girum imus nocte et consumimur igni*. Debord also envisaged a mass-market edition. Debord was something of an éminence grise at the Champ Libre publishing house, which published French editions of Clausewitz. In a 16 April 1972 letter to Gérard Lebovici, Debord points out the nineteenth-century (public domain) French translations of Clausewitz's writings. Guy Debord, *Correspondance* 4 (Paris: Arthème Fayard, 2004), pp. 541–542.

34 Jean-Jacques Lebel, "Dés-ir/Dés-ordre," *À pied, à cheval et en Spoutnik: Quelques écrits 1961–2009* (1977; repr., Paris: Beaux-arts de Paris, 2009), p. 62. Translation by author. The text was originally published in the catalog *Paris-New York*, Centre Georges Pompidou, Paris, 1977.

35 For a contemporaneous document of this involvement, see *Recherches*, no.

30 (November 1977), "Les Untorelli," which contains contributions by Félix Guattari and Franco "Bifo" Berardi, among others.

36 Kasper, *Spontis*, p. 154.

37 Gilles Deleuze and Félix Guattari, *Anti-Oedipus: Capitalism and Schizophrenia*, trans. Robert Hurley et al. (1977; repr., Minneapolis: University of Minnesota Press, 1983), p. 277.

38 As quoted in Gerald Raunig, "Nomadic Lines of Invention," *Transversal*, April 2008, https://transversal.at/transversal/0307/raunig/en; in Brian Massumi's English translation of *A Thousand Plateaus* (Minneapolis: University of Minnesota Press, 1987), a different version of the Jackson quote is given (p. 204).

39 The Invisible Committee, *Now*, trans. Robert Hurley (Los Angeles: Semiotext(e), 2017), p. 18.

40 Peter Osborne, "Theorem 4. Autonomy: Can It Be True of Art and Politics at the Same Time?," in *The Postconceptual Condition: Critical Essays* (London: Verso Books, 2018), p. 130.

41 Ibid., p. 131.

42 Teixeira Pinto, "Capitalism with a Transhuman Face," pp. 331–332.

43 An Architektur, "On the Commons: A Public Interview with Massimo De Angelis and Stavros Stavrides," *e-flux journal*, no. 17 (June 2010), https://www.e-flux.com/journal/17/67351/on-the-commons-a-public-interview-with-massimo-de-angelis-and-stavros-stavrides.

44 Stefano Harney and Fred Moten, *The Undercommons: Fugitive Planning and Black Study* (Wivenhoe: Minor Compositions, 2013), p. 64.

45 Jack McGrath, "What the New MoMA Misunderstands About Pablo Picasso and Faith Ringgold," *Frieze*, 18 October 2019, https://frieze.com/article/what-new-moma-misunderstands-about-pablo-picasso-and-faith-ringgold.

46 Arlene Dávila, "In Memoriam of the Art World's Romance with Diversity," *Hyperallergic*, 17 April 2020, https://hyperallergic.com/556290/in-memoriam-of-the-art-worlds-romance-with-diversity.

47 See Collectivize Facebook, https://collectivize.org.

48 On organizing/socializing AI, see Dan McQuillan's contribution in this volume.

49 "Instituting otherwise" has been an ongoing inquiry into the questions of infrastructure for art, research, and social action throughout the practice of BAK, basis voor actuele kunst, Utrecht, since its inception.

50 Raymond Williams, *Marxism and Literature* (Oxford: Oxford University Press, 1977), p. 123.

51 Ibid., p. 126.

52 Ibid.

53 See Ekaterina Degot and David Riff, eds., *Volksfronten/Popular Fronts: Steirischer Herbst '18 Reader* (Berlin: Hatje Cantz, 2019).

54 Jodi Dean, "Four Theses on the Comrade," *e-flux journal*, no. 86 (November 2017), https://www.e-flux.com/journal/86/160585/four-theses-on-the-comrade/. See also Jodi Dean, *Comrade: An Essay on Political Belonging* (London: Verso Books, 2019), p. 14.

55 Dean, *Comrade*, p. 2.

56 Jonas Staal, "Transunions," Biennale Warszawa, 2019, https://biennalewarszawa.pl/en/biennale-warszawa-2019/trans-unie-transunions.

57 See Matthias Meisner, "Wie die ARD Verschwörungstheoretikern auf den Leim ging," *Der Tagesspiegel*, 21 April 2020, https://www.tagesspiegel.de/gesellschaft/medien/querfront-protest-vor-der-volksbuehne-wie-die-ard-verschwoerungstheoretikern-auf-den-leim-ging/25755124.html.

58 Mark Scott, "Russia and China Push 'Fake News' Aimed at Weakening Europe: Report," *Politico*, 1 April 2020, https://www.politico.eu/article/russia-china-disinformation-coronavirus-covid19-facebook-google.

59 Lisa Graves, "Who's Behind the 'Reopen' Protests?," *New York Times*, 22 April 2020, https://www.nytimes.com/2020/04/22/opinion/coronavirus-protests-astroturf.html.

60 Joshua Clover, "The Rise and Fall of Biopolitics: A Response to Bruno Latour," *Critical Inquiry*, 29 March 2020, https://critinq.wordpress.com/2020/03/29/the-rise-and-fall-of-biopolitics-a-response-to-bruno-latour.

61 Murray Bookchin, "Libertarian Municipalism: The New Municipal Agenda," *From Urbanization to Cities* (1987; repr., London: Cassell, 1995), http://dwardmac.pitzer.edu/Anarchist_Archives/bookchin/libmuni.html.

62 See Sven Lütticken "Toward a Terrestrial," *e-flux journal*, no. 103 (October 2019), https://www.e-flux.com/journal/103/291974/toward-a-terrestrial/. For Latour on the "Earthbound," see Bruno Latour, *Facing Gaia: Eight Lectures on the New Climatic Regime*, trans. Catherine Porter (Cambridge: Polity Press, 2017). For Danowski and Viveiros de Castro on "Terrans," see Déborah Danowski and Eduardo Viveiros de Castro, *The Ends of the World*, trans. Rodrigo Nunes (Cambridge: Polity Press, 2017).

Donald J. Trump
Sponsored • Paid for by **TRUMP MAKE AMERICA GREAT AGAIN COMMITTEE**

Dangerous MOBS of far-left groups are running through our streets and causing absolute mayhem. They are DESTROYING our cities and rioting - it's absolute madness.

It's important that EVERY American comes together at a time like this to send a united message that we will not stand for their radical actions any longer. We're calling on YOU to make a public statement and add your name to stand with President Trump against ANTIFA.

Please add your name IMMEDIATELY to stand with your President and his decision to declare ANTIFA a Terrorist Organization.

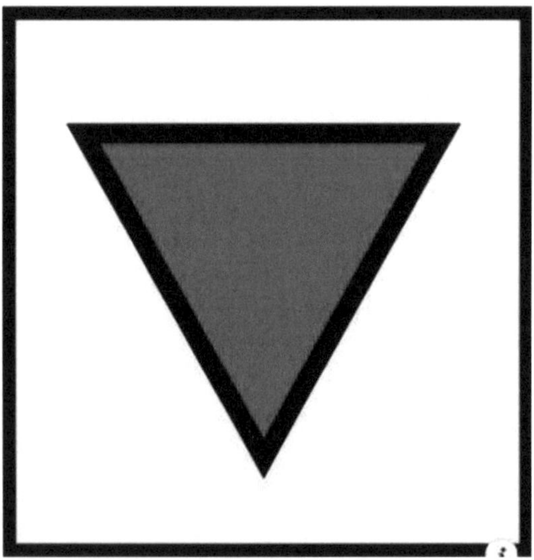

Donald J. Trump,
Facebook advertisement,
15 June 2020 (deleted)

Transfixing the Fascist Episteme

Tom Holert

1.

For many, particularly those engaged in anti-fascist organizing on the ground, the relationship of contemporary fascisms to knowledge, language, and cognition may not rank among the most pressing issues of the struggle. But the realms of the discursive and the epistemic assume increasing relevance for the development of effective left counterstrategies when we observe the alt-right's expanding use of digital culture in its bid for hegemony. Can a specific function be assigned to the politics of knowledge in the strategies of the contemporary far right? And is there any reason to believe that the epistemic politics of the right encroach on the field of contemporary art?

Increasingly invested in enterprises of discourse, education, research, theory, and investigation, the art world is undergoing a development that may be called *epistemization*.[1] In this context, we must reconsider notions of practice and action, political activism, the material–immaterial dichotomy, and the extent to which the ideological projects of "the knowledge society" and "cognitive capitalism" are being articulated in and through contemporary art.

Recognizing art and cultural practice's own past and present in enforcing the structures of cognitive capitalism may open room for a strategic reorientation. This not only pertains to contesting the dominant neoliberal systems of cognitive control and of epistemic as well as affective extraction, but also to the far-right knowledge systems so deeply ingrained in platform capitalism's epistemic regime. The epistemization of contemporary art is unthinkable without its integration into the very same infrastructures of digital capitalism that have also enabled the far right to flourish, bringing to its avail a host of algorithmic tools that gave it a heretofore unknown global reach.

The presence of digital fascism in contemporary art has become increasingly manifest with trends such as post-internet art, the celebration of "accelerationism," and exhibitions such as the 9th Berlin Biennale for Contemporary Art, curated by the editorial collective DIS in 2016, that pursued, in the words of curator Anselm Franke and cultural theorist Ana Teixeira Pinto, the "displacement of critical theory and the collapsing of the (ever-thinning) distinction between art and the creative industries.[2]

In certain parts of the art world, leaving the tacit consensus of Marxist criticality in contemporary art and theory led to an increased receptiveness toward right-wing ideas and tactics. By the end of the decade, these circles seemed ready to embrace, more or less explicitly, alt-right and neo-fascist postures.[3] Favoring creepy scandals and excitable speech, public secrecy and half-witted ressentiment, the algorithmic infrastructure of social media has been essential in crafting platforms and interfaces by which fascist thought can be relayed across the most heterogeneous social milieus and discursive arenas, contemporary art being only one (and particularly fractured) nodal area among them. But it is not simply the algorithmic circulation of alt-right and neo-fascist ideas, memes, and coded terminology that promulgate the advent of a fascist episteme. Its construction also requires the styles, ethics, and strategies of right-wing discourse, the specifics of its language, rhetorics, and epistemology, originating in a hoary (and horrific) tradition of reactionary and fascist cognition, in the very "epistemological chaos" that, in the words of historian Jill Lepore, "is the only air that totalitarianism can breathe."[4]

2.

In the months and years following 2015 and the so-called refugee crisis, on the instrumentalization of which the gains of the far-right political party Alternative für Deutschland (AfD) has largely been built, "talking to the far right" (*mit Rechten reden*) became an earnestly pondered, purportedly palliative measure across a disoriented left in Germany.[5] Increasingly concerned with the demise of open conflictual debate (*Streitkultur*), writers and journalists displayed hermeneutical and psychological interest in their right-wing counterparts (who they exoticized in the process), fascinated and appalled by the *vox populi* of those who loudly and persistently complained that they couldn't have a say and that their opinions wouldn't count, and even more by those voices and personalities who were considered to embody the intellectual avant-garde of the neo-fascist movement.

The public debate in Germany has morphed significantly, reactivating old patterns of fascist discourse and emulating more recent models of far-right electoral victory, such as the campaign for Donald Trump designed by Steve Bannon. Now German media, from public television to social networks, is populated increasingly by the vulgarisms and resentments of far-right memes. Annoyingly (and confusingly), alt-right factions such as Pegida and the Identitarian Movement trail from open hate speech to the coded lingo of cryptic allegations and back again. In close readings of the language of AfD politicians, literary scholar Heinrich Detering has instructively traced "the manipulative rhetoric of assertions and elusions" and the tactical linking of pathos and banality in speeches and interviews among the "parliamentary Right."[6] AfD and its followers have absorbed Antonio Gramsci's theory of cultural hegemony, even if the protagonists never read a line of the Italian anti-fascist militant. The left, or what is being represented (or rather, ridiculed) as such in the media, not least the newspapers and television shows deemed "filthy left-green" (*linksgrün versifft*) by the right, has geared into constant defense mode and self-blaming rhetoric—guided by the vain hope that facts, arguments, and discursive ethics might ultimately prevail.[7]

Such allegedly naive, yet symptomatic performances of clickbait journalism—parading, in full oblivion of its complicity, as the righteous demonstration of investigative ethics—also greatly contributed to a growing cultural legitimacy of the far-right scene. In their various media outlets, journals, streaming sites, and Facebook groups, the intellectuals of the German far right conduct what they call "metapolitics" (*Metapolitik*), following the French extremist philosopher Alain de Benoist, who since the 1970s almost single-handedly supplied the Western European neo-fascist scene with a theoretical framework for a polished version of anti-liberal thought.[8] Metapolitics, in Benoist's use of the term, is a sort of reasoning about key concepts such as state (*Staat*), people (*Volk*), and nature (*Natur*) which, according to its protagonists, should serve as building blocks of the present and future far-right intellect.[9]

Aimed at undermining and ultimately demolishing the liberal consensus about cultural diversity, freedom of expression, and an official restraint with regard to nationalist gestures (which is still the rule, despite structural racism and nationalist conservativism), these measures haven't achieved anything substantial in terms of policy making or legislation yet. They do, however, contribute to an atmosphere of anxiety through the noise they produce.

It was long expected that Pegida and AfD would eventually self-immolate, as had happened in the more recent German past when neo-fascist parties such as Nationaldemokratische Partei Deutschlands (NPD), Die Republikaner (REP), and Deutsche Volksunion (DVU) grew to a considerable size in the 1960s, 1980s, and 1990s, respectively, yet never made their successes sustainable due to internal conflicts and/or utter incompetence. This time, however, things are different. The AfD reigns supreme in the news, its politicians are busy performing victimhood for suffering "antidemocratic" mobbing by the media and attacks by anti-fascists, while they work social media as efficiently as no other party, expertly shifting, expanding, closing, and re-dressing the Overton window, like good students of strategists such as Bannon, Brad Parscale, and Dominic Cummings, who have coached Trump, Jair Bolsonaro, and Boris Johnson into power.

A major field of the far right's operation is located at the intersection of the epistemic and the affective: the realm where intellect becomes inseparable from emotion, rational from irrational, virtue from vice. This spot where an individual's ideas and beliefs are manufactured and shaped features prominently among the phantasmatic fixations of the right. Cummings, for one, the political strategist who conducted the 2016 Vote Leave Brexit campaign with unheard brazenness, is apparently "obsessed with propaganda" and determined to "build an army that is programmed to think like him."[10] The amount of brainwashing that seems to be going on in these circles is telling in more than one respect. It bespeaks a bewildering investment in the cognitive dimension of contemporary politics on all sides, a fixation on the brain that is conceived of as an object of speculation, an arena of electoral campaigning, a target (or resource) of data modeling, neuro-marketing, and digital messaging, but also as the site or non-site of power per se. And it doesn't have to be brilliant minds and brainy persons taking the seats of power or being placed in this or that target group or demographic. Rather, it is the brain in its material concreteness and plasticity, as well as in its substitutability by way of digital-algorithmic abstraction that counts. This brain is deliberately conceived of as machinic, a matrix of irrational choice whose contingency has become ever-more calculable and measurable by the ways of social media data analysis.[11]

Provocation and propaganda coalesce in the right's indiscriminate use of pseudo-rationalizations and para-arguments—for example, in posing as an "alternative" while identifying their "resistance" (*Widerstand*) with that of anti-fascists such as Sophie Scholl of the White Rose group in Nazi Germany.[12] Adding to such distortions and appropriations of historical fact the co-optation and inversion of the lexicon of the liberal left (most recently, for example, "resilience" has been built into their parlance), the new fascists steadily deploy a conceptualist approach by which they aspire to *Geistesherrschaft*, a hegemony of the spirit.[13]

3.

These ideological-epistemic activities and discursive-cognitive politics participate in a "larger geopolitical struggle of disinformation" through white supremacist forums and websites, extra-parliamentary networks on social media, as well as state-run media outlets pursuing a political agenda.[14] Things have reached a point where the far right has developed into something at the scale of an *episteme*. Dominating the discourse from the fringes, its strategists have learned from the history of the left, and particularly from the event of 1968 with all its political, social, and cultural repercussions. One of the most important lessons: you have to redesign, with all available means, the structures of feeling and thinking of the populace.

In retrospect, it becomes apparent how in the years leading to 1968 elements of an analytic of the fascist episteme began to surface and to coalesce. In *The Order of Things* (1967, trans. 1970), Michel Foucault modified the semantics of the Greek word *épistémè* (knowledge) to give it the sense of a historical, but non-temporal, *a priori* that grounds knowledge and its discourses and thus represents the condition of their possibility within a particular historical age, such as the "classical episteme" of the seventeenth and eighteenth centuries. An episteme defines the "conditions of possibility of all knowledge, whether expressed in a theory or silently invested in a practice."[15] Subsequently, Foucault would multiply the monolithic and universalizing episteme, acknowledging the coexistence and interaction of a plurality of epistemes at a time. Later on, he defined the episteme as "the strategic apparatus (*dispositif*)" which "makes possible the separation, not of the true from the false, but of *what may* from *what may not* be characterized as scientific."[16]

Through linking the concept of the episteme, defined as the normative framework in which (scientific) truth claims can be made, to the concept "fascism," we acknowledge the necessity of considering fascism in its generic rather than historical sense. That is, to consider fascism not only in terms of a political and social practice or system, with the attendant ideology or *Weltanschauung* (worldview), but as something more pervasive: as a kind of knowledge or epistemic modality that cannot be confined to the realm of explicit fascist doctrine.

Separating what may from what may not be characterized as scientific is a constant operation conducted by the discourse of the far right, particularly when it denigrates claims to scientific truth. It is therefore not a question of the denial of knowledge and truth altogether. Rather, the more the far right distrusts and depreciates knowledge, the more the epistemic seems to be at the heart of its project.

In 1967, Theodor W. Adorno gave a talk on the far right that was rediscovered in 2019 and found unexpected success as a bestseller in Germany. Adorno, like many of his contemporaries, alarmed by the rise of the neo-Nazi party NPD after its founding in 1964, underlined that not all elements of fascist ideology are simply untrue, "but the truth serves a false ideology, and the real feat of defense is essentially to impale (*aufspießen*) the abuse of the truth for the sake of the untruth, and to fight it."[17] Adorno further sketched a basic discursive strategy in which the far right uses truth by systematically distorting it:

> The most important method to put the truth in the service of untruth is to edit and isolate the observations that are true or correct as such, to take them out of context, for example in saying, "under Hitler we were well off, until he started this stupid war," without realizing that the entire economic boom of the years from 1933 to 1939 was possible only due to the hectic war economy that was the precondition of the preparation of the war.[18]

In Adorno's view, the lie starts where facts are displaced and used in an intellectually illegitimate, unethical manner, while a claim to truth, or in Foucault's terms, to "scientificity," is upheld. The far right, however, both persistently rejects *and* claims scientificity for its own statements and propositions. Science is distrusted, suspected of being biased and ideologically unreliable. But referring to science comes in handy whenever a claim about demographic developments, immigration, tax spending, or such like is in need of being asserted and supported.

But what if truth is incompatible with politics as such? In the same year when Adorno gave his talk, Hannah Arendt raised the question of truth and politics in more general terms. She mentioned the "brutally elementary data" of undisputable historical facts.

> It is true, considerably more than the whims of historians would be needed to eliminate from the record the fact that on the night of August 4, 1914, German troops crossed the frontier of Belgium; *it would require no less than a power monopoly over the entire civilized world*. But such a power monopoly is far from being inconceivable, and it is not difficult to imagine what the fate of factual truth would be if power interests, national or social, had the last say in these matters. Which brings us back to our suspicion that it may be in the nature of the political realm to be at war with truth in all its forms, and hence to the question of why a commitment even to factual truth is felt to be an anti-political attitude.[19]

Political wisdom would thus be inconceivable without its deprecation of truth. Truth, in Arendt's view, is politics' neglected other, incompatible with any efficient way of doing the latter.

Factual truth in particular, as Arendt emphasizes, has always been difficult to maintain since "facts have no conclusive reason whatever for being what they are; they could always have been otherwise, and this *annoying contingency* is literally unlimited."[20] That is why "factual truth is no more self-evident than opinion, and this may be among the reasons that opinion-holders find it relatively easy to discredit factual truth as just another opinion."[21]

Denouncing truth and cloaking lies in "truthiness" are two ways of proceeding in politics, regardless of orientation. But what if a certain obsession with factual truth and with a modality of an inverted truth-speaking is exactly what attains to the epistemic politics of the far right?

The peculiar attachment of fascism to speaking the truth as if it were just another kind of political lie has been brilliantly pinned down by Alexandre Koyré, a philosopher and historian of science, i.e., an expert in knowledge systems. In 1945, after living for several years in New York, teaching at the New School for Social Research (the "university in exile"), Koyré published an article on political lies in the journal *Contemporary Jewish Chronicle* in which he theorized the "open conspiracy," the public secrecy of a fascist politics of the lie.[22] Koyré argued that the enforced publicness of the act of lying in fascism becomes an epistemological limit case, but he did not stop at asserting a crisis of epistemology in general. Instead, he opened an entirely new set of concerns with regard to the epistemology of fascism, which for him was linked to a "given conception of man, an anthropology." Koyré argued that although fascist anthro-epistemology despises "the intuitive intellect, theory, the *nous* of the Greeks," this "totalitarian anthropology" does in fact fully acknowledge "discursive reason and rationalization."[23]

This is a compelling way of reading the fascist relation to knowledge and reasoning. Koyré didn't take refuge in the simplistic denial of epistemological purchase on the part of fascism; he was convinced that it should not be mistaken as the rule of the stupid nor reduced to neo-mythic murmur and utter anti-rationalism. Rather, he contended, fascism is grounded in an *anthropological* distinction between strong and weak modes of thought, between the abstractions of reason "in its highest forms," which fascism "abhors," and the crucially *operative* epistemics of "discursive reason and rationalization."

I would like to understand Koyré as saying that fascist epistemology is determined by a relentlessly goal-oriented reason and is thus continuous with the "instrumental reason" first theorized by Max Horkheimer in the 1940s and further developed by Jürgen Habermas and others.[24] For Horkheimer, *instrumental* reason was the technocratic corruption of *practical* reason in the sophisticated process of strategic choice of means to an end. Such operative notion of reason or knowledge, in its most vicious, violent form, is an essential element of the historical fascist episteme. In contemporary algorithmic decision-making, in the preemptive, strictly binary, biased, geometrizing, racializing abstractions of AI, theorized by Ramon Amaro, James Bridle, Dan McQuillan, Matteo Pasquinelli, Antoinette Rouvroy, and others, this operationality of thought has entered its next level. While fed with epistemic and ideological presumptions originating in human cognition, these systems become increasingly autonomous and disconnected from any human agency.

In Koyré's terms, it is also the full embrace of and identification with such operative reasoning that defines an "anthropological" hierarchy. The totally voluntary yet seemingly natural difference is drawn between an elite of fascist technocrats/rationalists on the one hand and the masses who either succumb to the lure of non-efficient liberal thought (to be prohibited at all costs) or to the temptations of irrationalism (which, as is well known, perfectly matches with elitist fascist intellectualism), on the other.

More recently, Robert O. Paxton arrived at a similar conclusion, when he stated that "fascism's radical instrumentalization of truth explains why fascists never bothered to write any casuistical literature when they changed their program, as they did often and without compunction."[25]

Paxton emphasizes the lack of any consistent theoretical base or program on which fascism stands. Adorno, in his 1967 lecture, made quite clear how fascism has never been "a really structured theory" but rather has to be understood as a "*sous-entendu*," a non-conceptual practice (*begriffslose Praxis*). "In contrast," Adorno continued, "the spirit [*Geist*], as it is tangible in theory, is placed as something of a secondary order. And it is exactly this [asymmetrical relation between non-conceptual practice and theory in fascism] that provided these movements ideologically with the kind of flexibility that can so often be observed. Other than that, it is a feature of the present spirit of the time [*Geist der Zeit*]."[26]

Now, it strikes me as a productive coincidence that Adorno and Foucault, writing at almost the same time (1966/1967)—the latter trying to read and classify the occidental, modern knowledge systems like an ethnologist of Western culture, the former trying to "transfix," or prepare for close study, the illogical patterns of 1960s far-right discourse—both grappled with concepts that were meant to enable them to speak about a historically specific and generalizable framework that regulates what is intelligible and acceptable (and what is not) in terms of thought and reasoning. Foucault's term "episteme" is interestingly refracted in Adorno's "spirit of the time," and it could be argued that Adorno saw the discourse of the far right as thoroughly permeating the episteme of postwar Western Europe.

4.

The thesis that fascist ideology was (or is) deeply ingrained in the totality of social cognition was probably most famously posited by Zeev Sternhell, an Israeli political scientist and historian whose work has considerably stirred up the debate around twentieth-century fascism with the publication of his book *La droite révolutionnaire (1885–1914): Les origines françaises du fascisme* (The Revolutionary Right (1885–1914): The French Origins of Fascism) in 1978. For Sternhell, the entire "Zeitgeist" of French prewar society was "impregnated" with fascist thinking. French fascism of the prewar years succeeded in permeating the public sphere. For historians and theorists of fascism such as Sternhell and Daniel Knegt, the epistemic dimension of fascism can only be "understood properly if it is taken seriously both as an ideology and as an intellectual phenomenon."[27]

Out of need for a precise transfixing of the contemporary episteme, the urban theorist and architectural critic Keller Easterling introduces the notion of the "superbug." She argues that "ideological declarations" have become "insufficient markers or activist tools because, with cross-purposes and discrepant messages, superbugs mix and confuse ideologies," operating on "latent potentials for accumulating power."[28] Constantly accumulating lies, this contemporary model of evil power has developed a multi-resistant and highly adaptive "kind of Teflon" that purposely undermines the very bases of rationality—"even lexical expressions seem to become physical forcefields decoupled from intentions." The resulting "toxic mixture of info-prop and reasoned dissent" produces the social cleavages and ideological polarities that made Brexit, Trump, Bolsonaro, and Narendra Modi possible, while the knowledge of everything that is wrong about them is abundantly available, at least in theory. However, as Easterling argues, the "superbug" effectively amplifies the "underlying binary" to ensure an "outcome opposite to one for which dissenters were agitating."[29] Through obfuscation, the far right gains its particular paradoxical clarity. Easterling's approach—her rendering of the contemporary lie and the superbug's operationality—could be seen as updating Koyré's, Arendt's, and Adorno's attempts at understanding the epistemic politics of the far right. Her reading of the methods of cultivating the lie in the public eye however doesn't stop at—the by now well-rehearsed—explanations and lamentations of far-right and alt-right distortions of truth.

Polarizations, divisions, and binaries no doubt shape the contemporary political landscape, and Easterling makes a strong warning to those who still believe in the efficiency of the plain counterattack—to the *anti-* of anti-fascism, anti-racism, etc. However, the hyperbolic superbug should also not be fetishized. As much as the term may help to better understand the way that the binary logic of AI and machine learning has patterned the operations of power, infrastructure, and contemporary prosumers' everyday selves, it also lends itself to easy cultural pessimism and political passivity.

That being said, Easterling's emphasis on disposition and latency, on the subterranean accumulation of power, as well as her attention to the becoming material of language—and therewith the decoupling of referent and meaning, human agent and algorithmic decision-making for the sake of arriving at unobstructed operationality—is a contribution to the task of giving relief to the contemporary fascist episteme. It renders that episteme more intelligible and thus potentially deconstructible.

5.

The "strategic apparatus" of episteme is being increasingly perceived as an issue of thinking—more precisely, of the control, censorship, and cancellation of the intellect or the mind itself. Among the entry points for this combined epistemization and neurologization of the political and cultural realm made readily available for far-right epistemic politics are the theorization and politicization of "framing," and in particular the neuro-linguistic concept of a "political mind."[30] Both have been promoted by George Lakoff, a cognitive linguist at the University of Berkeley, California, and former colleague of Noam Chomsky. Lakoff believes in the potential of neurolinguistics to fight right-wing politics and served as an advisor for the Democratic Party after its defeat in 2004, lobbying for "cognitive policies" and "framing campaigns." Books on "neuropolitics" and the power of metaphoric language, such as his 2008 *The Political Mind*, have altered the perception and understanding of social, political, and economic realities, supporting the suspicion that politics are to be increasingly considered as a matter of thinking (and feeling) on the material level of biochemistry and bioelectricity.[31]

If language is coming, via the discourse of neuroscience, to be considered less a tool of political strategy and manipulation in the face of more or less autonomous minds but rather as an instrument of neural reconfiguration and anthropological mutation on a large scale, we are facing a revival of mid-century mass psychology and George Orwell's dystopia of mind control (*1984* has become a reference for the alt-right), but also the collapse of the human self as the sovereign agent of potential change and emancipation. In this view, the contemporary subject is deeply immersed in a maze of attractions and repressions, a porous and endlessly navigable docking station for linguistic and algorithmic machines.

An earlier book by Lakoff dedicated to the notion of freedom, *Whose Freedom?: The Battle over America's Most Important Idea* (2006), was primarily inspired by the debate around freedom of speech and expression that turned into a key ideological weapon by United States conservatives in the 1990s and 2000s.[32] Here, Lakoff discusses issues of constitutional rights, philosophical concepts, political objectives, and artistic freedom, while being alarmed and dazzled by the right's capacity of taking advantage of the "neural turn" for which Lakoff's own research stands. Indeed, the old status quo has not just been disrupted by neoliberal-conservative think tanks and fascist lies but through the reorganization, the repackaging, and *recontextualization* of the human mind itself, its *ontological* displacement as pursued by a multiplicity of interested parties—some of them human and many, and increasingly more, non-human.

The right's appropriation of civil rights claims for the freedom of expression continues to have striking effects. In their hands, the trope of "free speech" turns out to be essentially about the regulation of thought or thinking, about fear-mongering allegations of antidemocratic disfigurations of the population's gray matter, that is, which the political establishment is supposedly covering up. References to the Orwellian "thought police," known from 1990s debates around "political correctness," persist today. There is a whole bundle of affects, ranging from depression and anxiety to euphoria and ecstasy, that are engendered and controlled by the invocation of threats against the freedom and capacity to think (and against the ownership of thought by the individual self). In some respects, the fear about having or not having the possibility or the right to speak one's own mind is the fear of losing out to machine learning and artificial intelligence, the fear of being robbed of the agency of thought and thus of labor and income.

While algorithms are taking over human intellectual labor, attention is diverted toward social and political groups accused of controlling, manipulating, and dispossessing authentic, autonomous thinking—something that many are, in fact, doing, with "framing" being one method of pursuing such disappropriation and distortion of independent thought. In order to render intelligible the relationship between platform capitalism's actual and acute apparatuses of cognitive and affective control and the far right's ideological fear of mind control, we must analyze, unpack, and subvert the proto-algorithmic operationality of this far-right production of untruth. This work of scrutiny should yield a better understanding of the far right's "impregnation" of the "Zeitgeist," as Sternhell has put it. One objective could be to decode the very system of knowledge that has become disjointed from human or non-machinic agency; this epistemic order actively organizes inequality and discrimination.

Rather than opting for a simplistic disavowal of the fascist episteme's violence, effectively deserting the culture wars would require engaging in the production of a set of critical skills and aesthetic languages that would enable actual transfixing. If the "non-fascist living" envisaged by Foucault is to be interpreted as a proposition to evade the pull of fascism and regain agency by dispelling it, by shrugging it off, it should be recognized that fascism itself is strongly "propositional" in character, grounded in "a vision about how the world should be."[33] Fascism thus actively and preemptively fights what stands in the way of its vision. What, then, would be the proposition in response? How best to evade fascism as a knowledge system, that is, as today's sturdy but shape-shifting mix of Silicon Valley-purchased, state-corporate algorithmic abstraction, digital economy, and fascist epistemic politics?

Franco "Bifo" Berardi suggests the "emancipation of knowledge-force" and an "ethical awakening" are "the only chance to defeat the neuro-totalitarian system in the making."[34] I share his basic assumption that contemporary power can be described as crucially exerted by means of neurotechnology. However, the "emancipation of the knowledge-force" Berardi envisions might be in need of some qualification in terms of both political organizing and epistemological reasoning. From workerist militant co-research to mobilizations around Black education, from feminist standpoint epistemology and situated knowledge to the epistemology of the closet, from subaltern and postcolonial to decolonial and indigenous epistemologies—the contemporary episteme is informed by the entangled genealogies of struggles centering on knowledge's access, distribution, and effects.

A large-scale conference on indigenous epistemologies and the artistic imagination, such as the one that took place at Museu d'Art Contemporani de Barcelona (MACBA) in October 2019, wouldn't have been conceivable in Western Europe or other centers of imperialism, say, 15 years ago.[35] Its possibility owes tremendously to the (unofficial) consortium of radical epistemologies mentioned above. Contemporary art's epistemic politics, in the best of all scenarios, provide the means and tools to both transfix and escape the fascist episteme.[36]

Elements of a toolkit for transfixing the fascist episteme can be found in the visual and theoretical practice of artists such as Hito Steyerl, Forensic Architecture, Tribunal NSU-Komplex auflösen (Tribunal "Unraveling the NSU Complex"), Cameron Rowland, Michael Rakowitz, and Jonas Staal. Their responses to the codes and language games of contemporary authoritarianism, far-right mobilization, and the prison-industrial complex are based on quite different formal and argumentative strategies. Yet, granted such differences, they share an interest in the techniques and conventions of critical and, at times, satirizing readings of hegemonic patterns as expressed, for example, in the antics and glossolalia of digital corporations, social media trolls, law enforcement agencies, or right-wing politics. This approach can play out through earnest analysis and explanation of the textual and visual production of the far right, as for example in Staal's exhibition and publication project *Steve Bannon: A Propaganda Retrospective* (2018), or through the investigations of the complicity of the German neo-Nazi terrorists of the so-called Nationalsozialistischer Untergrund (NSU), police, intelligence agencies, and a racialized society, as a whole conducted by the largely artist- and cultural-practitioner-driven Tribunal NSU-Komplex auflösen and Forensic Architecture.

These examples are reminiscent of Berardi's notion of an "ethical awakening" among knowledge workers, in contrast to, say, an *epistemic weaponizing*. And they recall the source text of the *Propositions for Non-Fascist Living* series at BAK (2017–ongoing): Foucault's 1977 preface to the English edition of Gilles Deleuze and Félix Guattari's *Anti-Oedipus: Capitalism and Schizophrenia*, which Foucault considered to be a treatise of ethics (in the Spinozean sense). Among the "essential principles" for an "art of living counter to all forms of fascism, whether already present or impending" that Foucault identifies in Deleuze and Guattari is the following: "Do not use thought to ground a political practice in Truth, nor political action to discredit, as mere speculation, a line of thought. Use political practice as an intensifier of thought, and analysis as a multiplier of the forms and domains for the intervention of political action."[37] In other words, a politics of knowledge should go both ways: integrating political action and the action of thought. If fascists understand this, we should as well.

1 See Tom Holert, *Knowledge Beside Itself: Contemporary Art's Epistemic Politics* (Berlin: Sternberg Press, 2020).

2 Anselm Franke and Ana Teixeira Pinto, "Post-Political, Post-Critical, Post-Internet: Why Can't Leftists Be More Like Fascists?," *Open! Platform for Art, Culture, and the Public Domain*, 8 September 2016, https://onlineopen.org/post-political-post-critical-post-internet.

3 See Angela Dimitrakaki and Harry Weeks, eds., "Anti-Fascism Art/Theory," special issue, *Third Text*, vol. 33, no. 3, (2019); Ana Teixeira Pinto and Kerstin Stakemeier, "A Brief Glossary of Social Sadism," *Texte zur Kunst*, no. 116 (December 2019), pp. 82–103.

4 Jill Lepore, "In Every Dark Hour," *The New Yorker*, 3 February 2020, p. 21.

5 Per Leo, Maximilian Steinbeis, and Daniel-Pascal Zorn, *Mit Rechten reden: Ein Leitfaden* (Stuttgart: Klett Cotta, 2017).

6 Heinrich Detering, *Was heißt hier "wir"?: Zur Rhetorik der parlamentarischen Rechten* (Stuttgart: Reclam, 2019), p. 19.

7 For a strong critical assessment of this expression see Margarete Stokowski, "Warum 'linksgrün versifft'?," *Der Spiegel*, 2 February 2019, https://www.spiegel.de/kultur/gesellschaft/rechte-sprache-warum-linksgruen-versifft-a-1252819.html.

8 See, particularly, the writings of the historian and independent journalist Volker Weiß, such as "Bedeutung und Wandel von 'Kultur' für die extreme Rechte," in *Handbuch Rechtsextremismus*, Fabian Virchow, Martin Langebach, and Alexander Hausler, eds. (Wiesbaden: Springer, 2016), pp. 441–469, and *Die autoritäre Revolte: Die Neue Rechte und der Untergang des Abendlandes* (Stuttgart: Klett Cotta, 2017).

9 There even exists "Metapedia," a far-right online-based wiki "alternative encyclopedia." See "Metapedia," Wikipedia, https://en.wikipedia.org/wiki/Metapedia.

10 A former staffer of Vote Leave, quoted in Sam Knight, "The Long Goodbye: In the Final Days of the Brexit Negotiations, the Future Became Visible," *The New Yorker*, 4 November 2019, p. 19.

11 A Tory think tank such as CAPX, which advocates "popular capitalism," actually speaks some truth about Cambridge Analytica's mind-reading and brain-washing agenda in plain sight, even or especially where it claims the opposite. See Andrew McKie, "Cambridge Analytica Aren't Mind-Readers or Brain-Washers," CAPX, 20 March 2018, https://capx.co/

cambridge-analytica-arent-mind-readers-or-brain-washers/.

12 Claus Leggewie, "Resist, Don't Reminisce!," *Eurozine*, 27 September 2018, https://www.eurozine.com/resist-dont-reminisce/.

13 Nicholas Michelsen and Pablo De Orellana, "Discourses of Resilience in the US Alt-Right," *Resilience: International Policies, Practices and Discourses*, vol. 7, no. 3 (2019), pp. 271–287.

14 Emmi Bevensee and Alexander Reid Ross, "The Alt-Right and Global Information Warfare," in *2018 IEEE International Conference on Big Data (Big Data)* (Seattle, WA: 2018), pp. 4393–4402, https://ieeexplore.ieee.org/document/8622270; Shannon Jones, "Mapping Extremism: The Network Politics of the Far Right" (PhD diss., Georgia State University, 2016), https://pdfs.semanticscholar.org/c471/0744d5136b4fcaad6eb2cbbd739f3458648a.pdf?_ga=2.180663847.1070579049.1579281473-839919582.1556454466.

15 Michel Foucault, *The Order of Things*, trans. A.M. Sheridan Smith (1970; repr., London and New York: Routledge, 1989), p. 168.

16 Michel Foucault, "The Confession of the Flesh," in *Power/Knowledge: Selected Interviews and Other Writings, 1972–1977*, ed. Colin Gordon, trans. Colin Gordon et al. (New York: Pantheon, 1980), p. 197. A few years earlier, in his inaugural lecture at the Collège de France in December 1970, Foucault had shifted terminology to a register that now seems somewhat more familiar, namely, from *episteme* to *discourse*, whose production "is at once controlled, selected, organized and redistributed by a certain number of procedures whose role is to ward off its powers and dangers, to gain mastery over its chance events, to evade its ponderous, formidable materiality." (Michel Foucault, "Order of Discourse," in *Language and Politics*, ed. Michael J. Shapiro [Oxford: Blackwell, 1984], p. 109.) However, for reasons that may become more palpable further on in this text and which are more generally bound to the term's intimate relation to knowledge and cognition, I would here like to stick to, making a few amendments, Foucault's *episteme* rather than *discourse*.

17 Theodor W. Adorno, *Aspekte des neuen Rechtsradikalismus*, with an afterword by Volker Weiß (Berlin: Suhrkamp, 2019), p. 39. Translation by author.

18 Ibid.

19 Hannah Arendt, "Politics and Truth," *New Yorker*, 25 February 1967, reprinted in *Truth: Engagements Across Philosophical Traditions*, José Medina and David Wood, eds. (Malden, MA: Blackwell, 2005), pp. 295–314, here p. 302.

20 Ibid., p. 304.

21 Ibid.

22 Alexandre Koyré, "The Political Function of the Modern Lie," *Contemporary Jewish Chronicle*, vol. 8, no. 3 (June 1945), reprinted in *October* 160 (Spring 2017), pp. 143–151. On Koyré and the lie in politics, see also Martin Jay, *The Virtues of Mendacity: On Lying in Politics* (Charlottesville, VA: University of Virginia Press, 2010), pp. 135–139, and John Keane, *Power and Humility: The Future of Monitory Democracy* (Cambridge: Cambridge University Press, 2018), pp. 180–183.

23 Koyré, "The Political Function of the Modern Lie," p. 150.

24 See Max Horkheimer, *Eclipse of Reason* (Oxford: Oxford University Press, 1947).

25 Robert O. Paxton, *The Anatomy of Fascism* (New York: Alfred A. Knopf, 2004), p. 18.

26 Adorno, *Aspekte des neuen Rechtsradikalismus*, pp. 40–41.

27 Daniel Knegt, *Fascism, Liberalism and Europeanism in the Political Thought of Bertrand de Jouvenel and Alfred Fabre-Luce* (Amsterdam: Amsterdam University Press, 2018), p. 16.

28 Keller Easterling, "Where Activism Fails and How We Can Reformat It. Activism in the Age of the 'Superbug,'" *Frieze*, 24 October 2019, https://frieze.com/article/keller-easterling-where-activism-fails-and-how-we-can-reformat-it.

29 Ibid.

30 On the concept of neurologization see Jan De Vos, *The Metamorphoses of the Brain: Neurologisation and its Discontents* (Basingstoke, Hampshire: Palgrave Macmillan, 2016).

31 George Lakoff, *Why You Can't Understand Twenty-First-Century American Politics with an Eighteenth-Century Brain* (New York: Viking, 2008).

32 George Lakoff, *Whose Freedom?: The Battle over America's Most Important Idea* (New York: Farrar, Straus and Giroux, 2006).

33 Angela Dimitrakaki and Harry Weeks, "Anti-Fascism/Art/Theory: An Introduction to What Hurts Us," in "Anti-Fascism/Art/Theory," Angela Dimitrakaki and Harry Weeks, eds., special issue, *Third Text*, vol. 33, no. 3 (2019), p. 278.

34 Franco "Bifo" Berardi, "The Coming '17," *e-flux Journal* 78 (December 2016), https://www.e-flux.com/journal/78/82058/the-coming-17.

35 See Indigenous Epistemologies and Artistic Imagination. 1st International

Symposium, convened by Juan Vicente Aliaga and Anna Maria Guasch, MACBA, Barcelona, 25 October 2019, https://www.macba.cat/en/exhibitions-activities/activities/indigenous-epistemologies-and-artistic-imagination.

36 Contemporary art's epistemic politics should also be raising awareness (and wariness) of the impending dangers of the epistemological extractivism looming over events such as the mentioned conference, while fostering the radical, trans-local, and trans-epistemic solidarities needing to be pursued.

37 Michel Foucault, preface to *Anti-Oedipus: Capitalism and Schizophrenia*, by Gilles Deleuze and Félix Guattari, trans. Robert Hurley et al. (1977; repr., London: Continuum, 2004), p. xiv.

be(coming) media—Technofeminist Pasts, Presents & Potentials

Diana McCarty

Let's start at the end.
The end of a journey from Africa
to the Caribbean. The end of a journey
known as The Middle Passage.[1]
From the Gold Coast to the Island of Haiti,
a journey of once free people,
stolen, shipped around the world,
to be sold, to be told.

A little bit of hoodoo is never wrong.
And what would Legba[2] say?

Let's start at the end of that journey.
Those once free people
met other enslaved Africans, born free
or born into oppression, Free People of Color,
on that tropical island.

Those survivors of The Middle Passage
found their kin among the people on that island.
Among them: Lieutenant Sanité Bélair.[3]

Those survivors of The Middle Passage,
Those once free people, those born into slavery,
those women and those men,
those people in between.

With their heads and their minds and their bodies and their arms
and they took up arms and they fought for their freedom
and they won. Well, they lost and they won
and they showed it could be done.

They Say: they practiced voodoo.
They Say: they poisoned the wells of those that stole them,
that sold them, that told them.

They Say: *Madame Bélair* refused to have her eyes covered
when she was executed by the French.

The Haitian Revolution

And Word Travelled. By ship, by sea,
From Port au Prince to New Orleans.
The first refugee crisis in the United States of America,
whites fleeing an Independent Black Haiti.

Transmitted.
By bodies, brown bodies, white bodies, black bodies,
word of mouth, newspapers, telegraphs.
The drums in Congo Square.[4]
Word Travelled.

This table, that table . . .
Who heard which word,
and what did they do,
knowing what they knew?

They Say: Nat Turner, he heard.
They Say: Harriet Tubman, she heard.

General Tubman[5] and her allies:
With their heads and their minds and their bodies and their arms
and they took up arms and they fought for their freedom
and they won. Well, they lost and they won
and they showed it could be done.

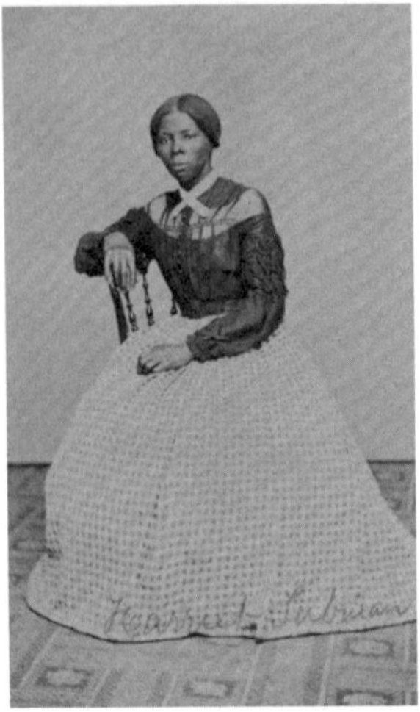

They Say: she carried a pistol.
They Say: she had visions.
And she fought and she won.

These particular bits of history have been partially forgotten, erased, recovered, repaired, tamed. But back then, this was news, big news. Who didn't talk about black ladies taking up arms to fight for their freedom?

Scenes in the Life of Harriet Tubman was published in the late 19th Century. Harriet was just released in cinemas around the world. In the future, her image will grace the face of American twenty-dollar bills.

Don't forget: this is about be(coming) media.
This Part is about TechnoFeminist Pasts,
but the Presents & Potentials are also present.

Word Travelled.

By ship, by rail—those workers—the twitter of their time.
It might have taken longer, but word travelled.

Carried, transmitted . . .
by letters, telegraphs, newspapers, books
—these words, these whispers, these rumors—
they were heard. In Paris; Saint Petersburg;
Kutaisi, Western Georgia . . .
The Far East of the Russian Czarist empire.

Who heard which word,
and what did they do,
knowing what they knew?

Gurians: They heard.
Even in that far flung backwater.
They heard and they did.

The Gurian Peasant Republic[6]

Now, the Gurians, they had the education and the literacy and all the reasons in the world to act on all those words. Villages had libraries, books, international newspapers and stories from around the world. Georgia might have been backwater, but it was also a crossroads: East, West, North, South . . .
ideas flowed in, through and out.
And, teenaged girls were in the mix.

They heard and they did.
They read and they wrote.
They ran printing presses
and distributed illegal papers.

They knew what to know.
And they taught. And they fought.

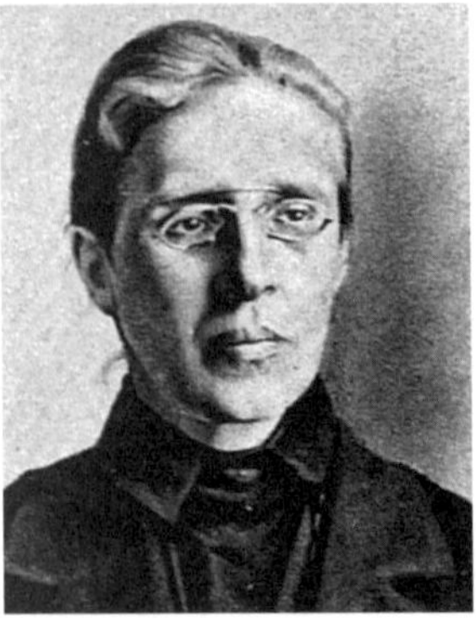

They shared what they knew
and they shared what to do.

All those militants: all those people.
Those peasants, those workers, those miners,
those women and those men
those ones in between.
Those teenaged girls.

They fought for their freedom.
With their heads and their minds and their bodies and their arms
and they took up arms and they fought for their freedom
and they won. Well, they lost and they won
and they showed it could be done.

And Word Travelled.

Who heard which word,
and what did they do,
knowing what they knew?

Lenin: he heard.
Maybe more importantly,
Elena Stasova[7]: she heard.
The Absolute–Lenin's Lady Laptop.
That keeper of codes, passwords, safe houses,
the keys, codenames, Bolshevik budgets.
The encrypted operations. She ran the Bolshevik center.
That holder of secrets. She heard.

They Say: she remembered, everything in great detail.
They Say: she never wrote anything down.
They Say: she trained others how to use codes.

There was even a Bank Robbery,[8]
an expropriation cum propaganda by deed:
a daytime job.

They Say: they carried grenades in their petticoats.
They Say: not a ruble was kept for themselves.
They Say: they took their secrets to their graves.

And Word Travelled.

Alexander Bogdanov[9]: He heard.
And what did he do, knowing what he knew?
This militant bolshevik, he did more than hear,
he did more than do: He told a tale, and oh, how he did tell!

RED STAR[10]: Set between revolutionary Russia
and Communist Mars. The red planet.

There on Mars, people lived in . . . well, a utopian society. There isn't time or space here to tell that tale, but it operated with art, gender, technology, work, love, life and the pursuit of happiness. It also had one hell of an organizational science to it. One hell of an idea about how technology could be used to better the lot of humanity. One hell of an imagination about what communication and information technology could do. Could be programmed to do.

Red Star is like a handbook for communist worlding.
Oh, Bogdanov was also an agronomist. Soil Science, baby.
Some say it was about the failed revolution of 1905 . . .
But if you know the codes . . .
my bet is on Guria.

That was 1908.
That's about a hundred years ago. A century and a bit . . .
Just a century and some change after the Haitian Revolution.

Word Travels.

By bodies, by songs, by beats,
by word of mouth, by letters,
by papers, by books.
Stories travel, sometimes just whispers,
sometimes just rumors.

This table, that table.
Who heard which word
and what did they do,
knowing what they knew,
hearing what they heard?

Don't forget: this is about be(coming) media.
It really is about Technofeminist Pasts, Presents & Potentials.
Don't fret, we'll get to cybernetics and Haraway.

So what is technology? In the Western tradition, techne is set as a differentiator from that which is human—its memory and history.

It is how and what the human transmits: through song, through movement, through language, though writing. Knowledge activated, materialized.

It is how and what the human imagines, renders, makes.
The apparatus, all that is not flesh. Something like that.

So what is Feminism?
A radical project that embraces race, class and gender in the struggle for . . . a better bakery, different recipes (maybe on Mars). A challenge to the modes of patriarchy. Of capitalism.

Centuries of struggles feed into what becomes a pivotal moment in what has made today.

All those militants: all those people.
Those survivors of the Middle Passage,
those born into slavery, those born into wealth,
those born into serfdom, those born into colonial rule,
those born into oppression, those that came before.

Those women and those men,
those girls and those boys,
those ones in between,
those ones that wanted more.

They fought for their freedom.
With their heads and their minds and their bodies and their arms
and they took up arms and they fought for their freedom
and they won. Well, they lost and they won
and they showed it could be done.

All that becomes a novel: not just a novel idea, but a science fiction novel that imagines an elsehere. Those militant women fighting for their freedom living on in the great in between. Now lost or footnotes on the pages of history, their names . . . disappeared. Almost a puff of smoke.

Still, Word Travels.

Warp Speed: Boats and trains and people and planes,
weapons and words travel more quickly.
To Latin America, to Africa, 1970ish . . .
Liberation Struggles.

Hortensia Bussi: she heard.
Who is she? She is a former teacher of history and geography that worked in Chile's Institute of Statistics. She also happened to be married to Salvador Allende. He, Raul Espejo, Fernando Flores and a few other Latin American socialist cyberneticians dreamt up Cybersyn: A kind of *Red Star*-inspired information hub that would manage the states' infrastructure—like a communist internet, operating in the interest of the people and not in the service of capital. Imagine that!

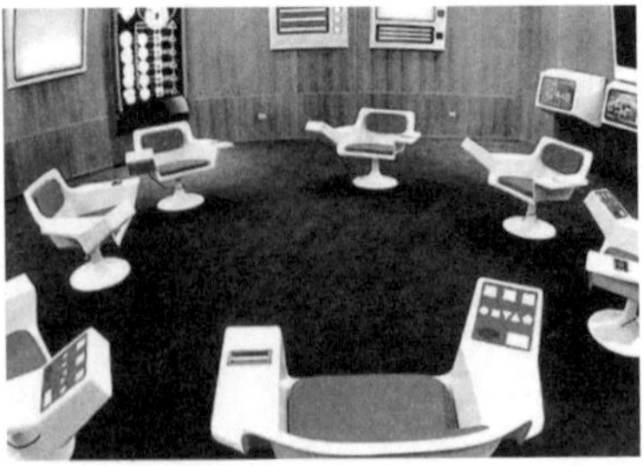

They Say: Wiener Read Bogdanov.
They Say: cybernetics started as a Socialist project.
They Say: Wiener did his most important cybernetic work in Mexico City.

Of Bussi, they say very little. My gut tells me she played a role. Time travel will tell.

Amílcar Cabral[11]: he heard.
There isn't time or space here to tell that tale,
the liberation of Guinea Bissau and Cape Verde.
Cabral, he was also an agronomist. . . . Soil Science.[12]

Anyhow, let's just say I have it on good information from an old militant, they read *Red Star,* back in the liberated zones, back in the jungle, back in the guerrilla schools.[13]

So Word Travels.

And what did they do, knowing what they knew?
What did Amílcar Cabral do, knowing what he knew?

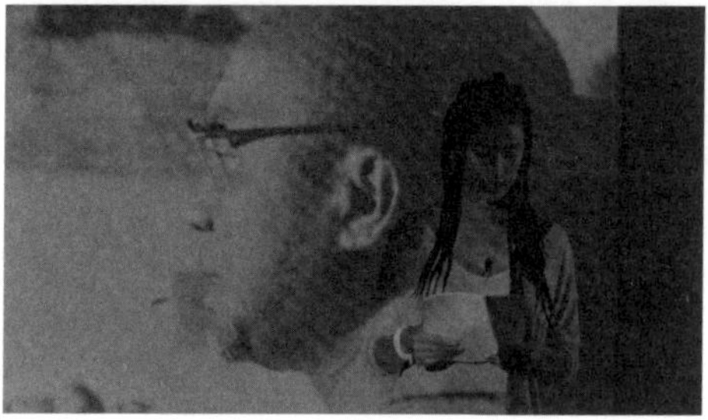

They Say: he knew the secrets of the soil.
They Say: he understood the value of a good education.
They Say: he ran a secret network of revolutionaries.

All those militants: all those people.
Those survivors of the Middle Passage,
those born into slavery, those born into wealth,
those born into serfdom, those born into colonial rule,
those born into oppression, those that came before.
Those women and those men,
those girls and those boys,
those ones in between,
those ones that wanted more.

They fought for their freedom.
With their heads and their minds and their bodies and their arms
and they took up arms and they fought for their freedom
and they won. Well, they lost and they won
and they showed it could be done.

Liberation struggles, civil rights, labor movements, and media: they are all in the mix. And cybernetics. A bit of nature, culture and technology. Word does travel. And people do, do.

Donna Haraway published “A Cyborg Manifesto” in 1985 in the *Socialist Review*. Just in time for the Great Injury to Communism. Then, in 1991, VNS Matrix gets in the mix:

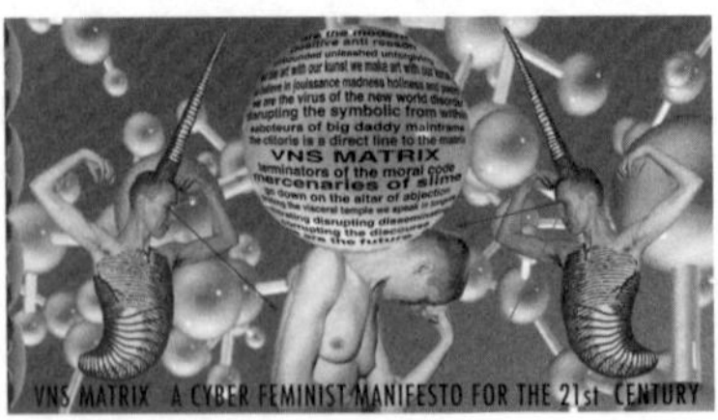

The Cyberfeminist Manifesto for the 21st Century
Generations of articulations of political ambitions called for different types of militancy and utilizations of technology: have both been the subject and object of technological innovation.

These shapeshifters are both real and fictional, material and immaterial. Their actions mean one thing in their own time, another in an other. They are (be) coming media. Medialized . . . idealized . . . fueling the imaginations and imaginaries of those who come after.

Word Travels.

By bodies, by songs, by beats,
by word of mouth, by letters, by papers,
by books. Language, body, voice, print,
technology, railroads, violence.
How is history inscribed and transmitted?

The carriers of ideas, memories half remembered,
almost forgotten. Some things get lost in the fine print,
old code, old codes. And some things, almost forgotten,
come back to life.

Remember: Haraway is writing in 1984, home computers are barely a thing, the internet is barely a thing. VNS Matrix, is busy while the web is almost becoming a thing: Social media, not even becoming a thing. Wireless internet, cell phones, smart things. . . . No Way.

WARP SPEED or fast forward to a couple of potentials:
Feminist Critiques of Science, Feminist Software Development, Cyberfeminism, Xeno-Feminism, check them out. Just ask the internet.

Militant Movements: The Zapatistas, the PKK and other left wing liberation movements all rely heavily on the media and technology for their work. Gender Liberation is a thing. . . . Don't forget, there are reading lists, education programs.

Along with her comrades, Fidan Doğan and Leyla Şaylemez, Sakine Cansız, a co-founder of the PKK was assassinated in 2013 in Paris.

They Say: she was inspired by Stasova.
They Say: she had a similar way of working.
They Say: some secrets died with her.

The coup du jour/soup du jour & allies in Berlin. It seems to be an intersectional multi-ethnic queer feminist collectivity. It appears that they operate anonymously through social media outing the white male hetero-normative art practices and politics in the Berlin and German art worlds.

They Say: it has the art world in a frenzy.
They Say: the campaigns can ruin reputations.
They Say: it is a secret group.

They use stickers, posters, letters, press releases and social media for their campaigns.
Whispers and rumors . . .

Word Travels.

Then there is Sci-Hub,[14] the first pirate website in the world to provide mass and public access to tens of millions of research papers. It is an illegal database of subscription based scientific and academic journals that was programmed by Alexandra Elbakyan.

They Say: she did it on her own.
They Say: she cannot travel.
They Say: it is used around the world.

So this is how solidarity works: over time, over space, for here and for there, for me and for mine, for you and for yours, for we and for ours. Kinship. Word travels, and it returns.

All those militants: all those people.
Those survivors of the Middle Passage,
those born into slavery, those born into wealth,
those born into serfdom, those born into colonial rule,
those born into oppression, those that came before.

Those women and those men,
those girls and those boys,
those ones in between,
those ones that wanted more.

They fought for their freedom.
With their heads and their minds and their bodies and their arms
and they took up arms and they fought for their freedom
and they won. Well, they lost and they won
and they showed it could be done.

be(coming) media. Technofeminist Pasts, Presents & Potentials is about how these words and actions and ideas and dreams collide.

This text and my research as a BAK 2019/2020 Fellow draw from two very long, ongoing projects: *Luta ca Caba inda* (the struggle is not over yet) with Filipa César, and *Burning Red*, with Franziska Kleiner. I'm deeply indebted to Sonia Borges, Wendy Chun, Valie Djordjevic, Seda Gürses, Kathy Rae Huffman, Grada Kilomba, Suzana Milevska, Alla Mitrofanova, Anjalika Sagar, Hito Steyerl, and Katalin Timar. So, as a straight cis woman, when I fall into "we," as I often do, it is to describe the collective work and ideas of a motley crew of time travelers and trouble makers—some time traveling trouble makers. In any case, I rarely travel alone, and I am always somehow in conversation with the ancestors, the friends, the comrades, and the cool cats. So I'm carrying and bearing the words and wisdom of many, not least the mini-mafia and the magic communists. I'm delighted to add my fellow BAK Fellows to this mix.

1 The Middle Passage refers to how enslaved Africans were forcibly transported across the Atlantic to the West Indies. Over three to four months, the enslaved people mostly lay chained in rows on the floor of the hold or on shelves that ran around the inside of the ships' hulls.

2 Papa Legba is a loa in the Vodou religion and voodoo belief system. He is known as Lord of the Roads, God of the Crossroads, and the Great Communicator. He is known to have the gift of all speech, being able to talk in any human language.

3 Sanité Bélair was a Haitian Freedom fighter and revolutionary, lieutenant in the army of Toussaint Louverture. She was an active participant in the Haitian Revolution, became a sergeant and later a lieutenant during the conflict with French troops of the Saint-Domingue expedition.

4 Congo Square provided the enslaved black population in New Orleans with a space to congregate, express spiritually, sing, dance, and play drums.

5 Harriet Tubman was a US-American abolitionist and political activist. Born into slavery, Tubman escaped and subsequently made some 13 missions to rescue approximately 70 enslaved people using the network of antislavery activists and safe houses known as the Underground Railroad. During the American Civil War, she served as an armed scout and spy for the Union Army. In her later years, Tubman was an activist in the struggle for women's suffrage.

6 The Gurian Republic was effectively an autonomous region. It had its own

system of government, which consisted of assemblies of villagers meeting and discussing issues between 1902–1906. Formed out of a revolt over land grazing rights with decades old roots, it gained traction through the Georgian social democrats and during the 1905 Russian Revolution. The Russian imperial authorities were not able to reassert control until they used overwhelming military force.

7 Elena Stasova was a Bolshevik revolutionary and a specialist in "technical matters," such as creating false passports, organising escape routes, and making contact with sympathisers in the Russian army. She also taught new members how to encode and decode.

8 The 1907 Tiflis Bank Robbery was organized by Bolsheviks to fund their revolutionary activities. The revolutionaries attacked a bank stagecoach carrying Czarist currency and escaped with 341,000 rubles (equivalent to around 3.96 million US dollars..). in 2018).

9 Alexander Bogdanov was a Bolshevik agronomist, physician, philosopher, science fiction writer, and revolutionary. He invented "tectology," now regarded as a forerunner of systems theory. Bogdanov co-founded the proletarian art movement Proletkult and was its leading theoretician.

10 *Red Star* is Alexander Bogdanov's 1908 science fiction novel about a communist society on Mars.

11 Amílcar Lopes da Costa Cabral was a Bissau-Guinean and Cape Verdean agronomist, agricultural engineer, intellectual, poet, theoretician, and revolutionary. He was one of Africa's foremost anti-colonial leaders. Cabral led the Partido Africano da Independência da Guiné a Cabo Verde (PAIGC) guerrilla movement against the Portuguese government, which evolved into one of the most successful wars of independence in modern African history.

12 Filipa César (with Diana McCarty), "Meteorisations Reading Amílcar Cabral's Agronomy of Liberation," in "The Wretched Earth: Botanical Conflicts and Artistic Interventions," Ros Gray and Shela Sheikh, eds., *Third Text*, vol 32, no. 2–3 (2018), p. 256.

13 See Sonia Borges, *Militant Education, Liberation Struggle, Consciousness: The PAIGC education in Guinea Bissau 1963–1978* (Bern: Peter Lang, 2019).

14 The Sci-Hub website can be accessed at: https://sci-hub.tw/.

Images:
Page 80: Benjamin F. Towelson, *Portrait of Harriet Tubman*, 1868, photograph, courtesy of Library of Congress/Getty Images; p. 82: Unknown, Elena Stasova, ca. 1920, photograph; p. 86: Cybersync Operations room, 1971, courtesy Gui Bonsiepe; p. 87: Filipa César, Grada Kilomba, and Diana McCarty, *CONAKRY*, 2019, film still, courtesy the artists; p. 88: VNS Matrix, *A Cyberfeministmanifesto for the 21st Century*, 1992, billboard, courtesy the VNS Matrix.

The Promises of the Present

Bini Adamczak

When the Soviet Union imploded in 1990, many thought history had ended. Representative capitalist democracy had won forever. No one today really believes this anymore. In recent years, the ugliest undead have reentered the stage of history. Nationalist, fascist, and neo-Nazi movements, which many thought dead and buried, are now returning. Their ideologies, organizational structures, and methods of propaganda have been described many times before. But why are they returning now? What are the cracks in the conditions of the present from which they crawl out? And above all, why are they attractive? What promises do they make?

The return of European fascism far beyond Europe cannot be explained without reference to the recent crisis of the capitalist world economy. This was not only an economic crisis but a legitimation crisis of neoliberalism. Neoliberalism's promise was: "You alone can do it." It was a promise of freedom, wealth, and self-realization. "You can do anything," it said, "if you focus entirely on your career and family." This individual promise of success lost its appeal with the global economic crisis more than ten years ago. With the crisis came images of people moving out of their homes and living in tents, as in the United States, and news of people who could no longer pay their electricity and medical bills, as in Greece. All of a sudden, they were in debt, and instead of being in the middle of society, they were on the margins. There have always been stories like this. Yet, this did not occur in isolation, but on a massive scale, not staggered in time, but at the same time. These were not individual cases, and so this was not individual failure.

The Disintegration of Society

The crisis stimulated a realization that had long been repressed: the connection of the separated. As a result, it spread a certain insight that sociologists and statisticians had known for a while. In the last 30 years, some individuals had grown enormously wealthy, but for the majority of the population, wealth had not increased. Since economic growth in formerly industrialized nations was relatively low, despite all their business-friendly reforms, the wealth of the minority could only have come at the expense of the majority. In the US, for example, the share of the top 1 percent in overall social wealth had risen to the same extent as the share of the bottom 50 percent had fallen. But as long as no one saw themselves—or wanted to see themselves—as part of the poorer majority, this fact went unnoticed. A particular feature of the neoliberal era was the disintegration of society and its separation from the fate of the individual. A majority of people felt that the state of society would deteriorate in the future. At the same time, conversely, they were convinced that they themselves would be better off. With the economic crisis, however, more and more people realized that something must not be right here. If everyone was worse off, how could anyone be doing better?

What returned with the crisis of 2008 was, first of all, *society*—that which Margaret Thatcher claimed did not exist. "There are individual men and women and families," she said in the late 1980s, but no such thing called society. There were just gendered individuals competing with one another, and families into which these individuals could retreat, like a trailer camp—this is how the world looks in the neoliberal worldview. Millions of individuals went their own ways, telling each other at dinner parties that they had nothing to do with one another. This fantasy could only be maintained as long as the shop was still running. When the bubbles of speculation finally burst so too did the fantasy of individual autonomy. The state, which was supposed to stay out of everything except defense, now had to save the failed banks and indirectly provide their executive boards with their salaries. When it came to assuming liability, society was suddenly dug up again.

Many admirers of social democracy saw in this development a possible alternative way forward, culled from the recent past. The society that returned was said to be the society that had immediately preceded neoliberalism: the society of Fordism. Its promise then had a very different sound. Addressed to white males, it proclaimed: "Hold still, be diligent and obedient, and you will be better off than your father." It was a promise made with an eye toward the Soviet Union, a promise based on the exploitation of the Global South, the widespread exclusion of women, and the increased exploitation of migrant labor.

The high growth rates of the post-war economy allowed the Fordist promise to be maintained for several decades without affecting the relation between classes. Inequality yes, but a higher absolute baseline for all—that was the social democratic compromise. At the end of the 1960s, this compromise fractured simultaneously from several sides. In 1967, the world economy experienced its first major crisis in a long time, and shortly afterwards, social clashes broke out in many countries in the North, like those which had already long been raging in the South. The anti-colonial struggles for liberation that had challenged the world order reached the metropolises of West and East simultaneously in Paris and Prague, Berkeley, Berlin, and Belgrade. In the Global North, the broad movement showed that large sections of the population were unwilling to accept the exchange of freedom for security any longer. The social democratic promise of Fordism—belonging through subordination—lost its appeal.

Blair, Schröder, Hollande

Despite several attempts, this promise could not be rehabilitated even in the current crisis. This is partly because social democratic parties themselves had started dismantling social welfare in the 1990s—Tony Blair, Gerhard Schröder, and, after some delay, François Hollande. The protagonists of New Labour often came from the struggles of 1968 and had amalgamated the rhetoric of liberation with that of flexibilization. Once in power, their concern was less with alienation than with the nation. The flexibilization of labor markets and finance, along with tax cuts and welfare rollbacks, led to a recovery of profit rates. But the promised investment boom and rising growth rate, which could have enabled a return to the longed-for past, failed to materialize. At the beginning of the twentieth century, social democracy had abandoned its aspiration for overcoming capitalism; at the end of the twentieth century, social democracy abandoned even its claim to socially moderate it. First, it bet on the welfare state, and then on its destruction. It said farewell to the class struggle of its own accord. But social democracy is no longer needed for maintaining class compromise—without stable growth rates, such a compromise lacks an economic basis. That is why, despite the crisis of neoliberalism, social democracy is crashing in Europe wherever it was once strong.

There, where the individual promise of neoliberalism reveals itself to be a lie to the masses, and the collective promise of Fordist growth lacks any material basis, the nationalist right presents itself as a viable reaction to the crisis and the accompanying fears of downward mobility. It makes a tempting offer to a chosen section of the population: "Join us, and we will secure your standard of living at the expense of the weaker." This message is directed outward as well as inward. When the right carries out sexist, anti-Semitic, and racist attacks, it communicates to its followers another vision beyond the usual mockery, hatred, and contempt: the vision of a secure fortress of family, nation, and race.

The queer theorist John D'Emilio already made this discovery in the 1980s. He noted that anti-feminism, or the hatred of sexual minorities and gender self-determination, are not simply expressions of a lack of education or cultural backwardness but rather emerge from a fundamental contradiction within our basic social relations. Indeed, contemporary campaigns against sexual and gender self-determination use the notion of a healthy nuclear family that needs to be protected from outside threats. D'Emilio argued that the family in modern bourgeois society exists in a structurally precarious situation. In pre-bourgeois times, the family was able to provide for its members, but capitalism deprived it of central economic functions. Today, food is still prepared at home but no longer produced there, and clothes may be ironed at home but no longer sewn there. The family is a place of consumption and reproduction, but no longer of production. Historically, the role of the family has experienced a tremendous loss of relevance. At the same time, however, domestic labor continues to be socially necessary, and increasingly so with the dismantling of the welfare state; this includes raising children, caring for the sick and elderly, and providing security and shelter.

The wage for this labor, however, is not money but love, as the feminist Silvia Federici had already observed in the 1970s. On the one hand, the family is indispensable and therefore constantly praised—on the radio, in TV shows, and films—as a place of longing. On the other hand, the family has long ceased to have the power to fulfill the hopes that are placed in it. Under such high demands, it regularly collapses. In the Christian West, this can be seen every year during the Christmas season, but also through the fact that marriage continues to be the norm, even though the divorce rate is now 70 percent in large cities. The contradictory situation of the modern bourgeois family leads time and again to the frustration of the longing for security and belonging. And precisely in regard to this contradiction, the right offers scapegoats: abortion advocates, feminists, and queer people.

Masculinity, Germanness, Whiteness

Other core right-wing ideologies can be understood in a similar way. Christian Ernst Weißgerber, a German former neo-Nazi, responded to the question of what makes Nazi ideologies attractive by explaining that they "provide a security anchor against the uncertainties of the future," as they naturalize gender, nation, and race. Masculinity, Germanness, and whiteness appear irrevocable, quite differently than a lease agreement or employment contract. Here, the same contradiction arises as before: If my identity is actually secure, then how can I explain the persistent anxiety and fear that I have under crisis-ridden capitalism? The right-wing answer: it must come from outside—from migrants, refugees, and Muslims. Or from within—from those who undermine the nation, Jews above all, but also filthy green leftists. But fascism does not create security. Not for those whom it terrifies, of course, but not even for those to whom it seems to offer security. Its inner logic drives necessarily toward war.

The danger of fascism today is undeniable and truly global. It is unclear what promises can be put forth against it while the promises of neoliberalism and social democracy are in such deep crisis. In his book *Sapiens: A Brief History of Humankind* (2014), the Israeli historian Yuval Noah Harari answered the philosophical question of whether the history of humanity has a goal with a simple “yes.” Humanity aims for more and more unification. The Mayan and Roman empires already connected more people with each other than a single person could get to know in one lifetime. But those civilizations had no connections to each other, they did not even know of the other’s existence.

Today, the US, North Korea, and Iran rely on the same theories of physics, and it takes only nanoseconds to exchange their currencies. In this context, it becomes clear that various concepts inherited from the past no longer make sense. First of all, the concept of the nation. The global economy is intertwined to a new degree, as is the influence of the economy on global ecological systems. Climate change affects the entire planet and can only be mitigated by coordinated efforts across the world. Migration is similarly a global question. Questions of whether people from other continents should be allowed to come to Europe or the US are already wrong, if one assumes that they can only be answered by the people or the governments of Europe or the US. This contradicts the principles of democracy—after all, democracy means that decisions are made by those who are affected by them. The question of migration concerns people at the point of arrival as well as those at the point of departure, and especially those who move in-between. The principles of democracy permit no hierarchy here, and certainly no exclusion. Indeed, the French revolutionaries did not force the king to sign a declaration of *French* rights, the First Article of the German Basic Law does not say “the dignity of *Germans* is inviolable,” and the US-American Constitution does not begin with “all *Americans* are born equal.” The nation is always at odds with democracy. This was already true when these constitutions were drawn in the eighteenth century, but today the material conditions that supported the contradictions of the nation are eroding. The questions of ecology and migration are global questions, and so they can only be answered globally.

The System of Competition

Another concept of the past that no longer functions today is the capitalist economy. It was precisely the capitalist world market that accelerated the process, as described by Harari, of unifying humanity to an unprecedented level. But capitalism connects people only by separating them. The market only retroactively creates a link between supply and demand through the mediation of goods and money. Suppliers produce without binding agreements with consumers, and they compete with other suppliers. This system of competition forces private producers, under threat of bankruptcy, to expand their production more and more. Capitalism thus entails a constant compulsion to grow. Today, this compulsion to grow is reaching its ecological limit. It is no coincidence that the years with the largest reductions in carbon emissions were the years following the global economic crisis.

Capitalism also contains a crisis tendency in a more fundamental sense. The system of private production for the market means that it is only possible to determine after the fact whether demand actually exists for a product, and thus for the labor accompanying it. The central economic relations that connect people in global capitalism are thus necessarily precarious. Not only are employment and housing insecure under capitalism but even membership in society itself. That is why capitalist relations are fundamentally charged with fear, a fear that has been imbued with new power by neoliberalism. It is this fear to which the right reacts with the promise of irrevocable but exclusive belonging: to the race, to the nation, and to the family.

Here, we should build on an insight from D'Emilio: if anti-feminism and anti-queer hostility emerge from the contradiction between the ideological invocation of the family and its actual overload, then the material basis of sexist hatred can only be dissolved if alternative models to family and money relations are developed. The same goes for nationalism and racism: if they offer exclusive and armed security against the competition of the market, then they can only be countered through the reconstruction of our economic relations. Only an economy based on solidarity can effectively reduce generalized fear.

In Exchange for Subordination

The global economic crisis crisis of 2007–2008 severely damaged the neoliberal promise of individual success through competition in the market. Against this backdrop, there has returned the ugly promise of group success through competition among genders, nations, and races. In addition, the Fordist promise of enjoying growth in exchange for subordination cannot be repeated; in view of the imminent climate catastrophe, we know that further growth is no longer an option. Economists assume that the world economy will face new crises. The large public loans that were used to combat the last crisis will become the engines of the next crisis. None of the capitalist models—fascist, Fordist, or neoliberal—can give answers in this situation. In the end, they are all based on competition, whether as individuals or groups. Now that further growth is prohibited from an ecological point of view, cooperation must take the place of competition, just as democratic commons must take the place of private ownership of the means of production.

The hope of securing one's own privileges through the violent exclusion of others can no longer be realized under conditions of global interdependence. Real security does not consist in sleeping behind an alarm system, but in not having to be afraid of others. This is hardly possible as long as the basic relationships through which we are connected are based on indifference and competition. For this reason alone, the only promise that is still convincing today is the promise of universal solidarity that does not end at the borders of private property or the nation. Against the fear incessantly generated by the capitalist mode of production, this promise aims at true security—not the limited security of the few, but security for all.

Translated from German by Jacob Blumenfeld

From ReproModernism to ReproTechnoTribal (beta): A Disruption of Modernist Family Relations in Four Psycho-Realist Diagrams

Transformella
cared for by Johannes Paul Raether[1]

On the following pages **I-as-us**[2] document four Repro-Communal Diagrams. They present actual, potential, and speculative Repro Architectures that we have analyzed and re-developed over recent years. Usually they are used on-site in everysite's **Ikeality,**[3] but they can also be deployed in derivative narrations of our Repro Research Rituals, such as the one held at BAK in the framework of *Propositions #9: Deserting from the Culture Wars.* For Us-as-I, they function as attempts to map existing and excavate forthcoming Repro-Tribal Structures, which will ultimately overgrow nuclear and extended family concepts of the twentieth century and confuse their-as-our sense of Repro-Normality.

Us-as-I store them on my-as-our **Data Body,**[4] an inter-identity device that contains all of our psycho-realist language devices—a heap of data as a digital pile of scraps and notes, fragments of books, lengthy texts, complicated essays, and incomprehensible languages (which are self-made or appropriated). A Data Body, instead of a Bio Body, functions therefore as my "memory" in a fragmented and artificial identity, which speaks through multiplicities.

I-as-us think of these diagrams as a subset of "language devices." These can be various forms of text, spoken word, poetry, or diagrams that help to recalibrate Common Reality and make visible my-as-your decentered and fragmented subjectivity. With the diagrams, I-as-us propose to excavate a reconstructed and potential psychic real. If you would prefer a slightly more down-to-earth characterization, they can also function as a vantage point from which to gaze into a completely different social structure: a society of beings that is situated beyond the horizon of capital and gender, and beyond the current human ideas of kinship that have colonized the planet.

Of course, there are many dangers in unleashing repro-tech from its tight ideological geo-fencing and its generational time-fencing. We need to be aware that non-fascist living is something that needs to be reimagined again and again. But the actual peril of a rising fascism lies in liberal eugenics and white repro-colonialism. It is linked to total competition and increasing neoliberal and biopolitical individualization. The result is the pressure that people feel to enhance their Reproduct—their own child—and their proprietary reproductive relations. The way that property relations bleed into life itself: this is the actual fascist specter that's haunting not just Europe, but the planet. And the reproduction of human life itself is haunted by property relations.

ReproModernism

nuclear family

Human	ontological	Human
Adult	legal	Adult
Monogamous	romantic	Monogamous
Gendered	natural	Gendered
♀	heterosexual	♂
In-body	local	In-body
Biological	genetic	Biological
Fertile	medicinal	Fertile
Monotheist	religious	Monotheist
Productive	economic	Productive
Alive	immediate	Alive

Child

Alive
Human

Gendered
Fertile

1.

In ReproModernism the family is nuclear. Its relations can be described as biological, genetic, local, and natural. They force the gendering of individuals, becoming the container for "natural" fertility and an important vector in sexualizing relations among human adults. The diagram shows reproductive relations as undisrupted parallel lines stacking the status quo, which in various planetary societies is both past and present. Consequently the connections are drawn as direct lines of reproduction from one human subject to the other. As much as it is a horizontal connection between subjects and their in-body nuclei, it's a relation with formal hierarchies and coherently gendered entities. The creation of a child by "natural," "local," and "immediate" reproduction is, to many people, the most stable, robust, and even transhistorical form of reproduction and they deny ReproModernism's apparent remnants of the Holy Family—and therefore its ideological, religious, and monotheistic historical implications, and the aesthetic and political limitations that come with this normalized framing. I-as-us will merely use this diagram as a starting point to hopefully show potentials for dissolution and reconfiguration.

ReproPostModernism

patchwork family

Human — Human — Human

Adult — Adult — Adult

Biological — genetic — Biological

XGamous — romantic — XGamous

XGendered — XGendered – selfdetermined – XGendered

⚧ — x sexual — ⚧ — heterosexual — ⚧

Off Body — social — In-Body — local — In-Body

N.N — Fertile — medicinal — Fertile

NON Reproductive — NN — Productive — economic — Productive

inherited — legal — coincidental

Reproduct

Human
Child
XGendered
Fertile

2.

The repro-structure in this second diagram is a description of a materially and biophysically unchanged set of relations—which have, however, morphed socially. Since ReproModernism and its feudal and religious implications have become a somewhat ghostly, petrified, and outdated version of what is perceived as "normal" in many ReproRealities of the North West this represents an *übergangsszenario* (a transitional model of reproduction) that connects ReproModernism and Reprovolution by a ReproPostModern condition.

As in-body, cellular, genetic, local, and immediate reproduction remains the standard while social relations diffract, the diagram represents certain mobilizations as missing links in a grid. Impartial parallel lines signal a mobilization of social parenting forms, trans-subjective and trans-familial forms of care, and a renewed interest in proto-tribal or extended family structures. Formerly necessary relations, vectors, or connections might be disjointed and stretched across multiplied reproductive relations, mostly in time. A relation might still be romantic or sexual, but the reproduct might be inherited, or taken in across the grid from more than one social relation.

Yet, while social relations get more complex, biophysical relations remain bio-technologically stable. Some of the stacked connections still form an important vector in sexing and gendering individual entities, yet they are not as formative, allowing other subjectivities to emerge into the context of human reproduction, while they are still formed entirely by human adults. Machines or non-human surrogates are not even considered part of the technologies of reproduction. There is a common term for emotional and sexual relations that start to divest from reproduction: serial monogamy. This represents a socially polymorphic reproductive model which some social scientists call the patchwork family model. It is still nuclear, but nuclear in disjointed time. It is also important to note that all of the totipotent stem cells remain within the subject's body, represented by the dot in the center of the symbol for the biologically sexed body.

Reprovolution

within the limitation of reprotechnological determination

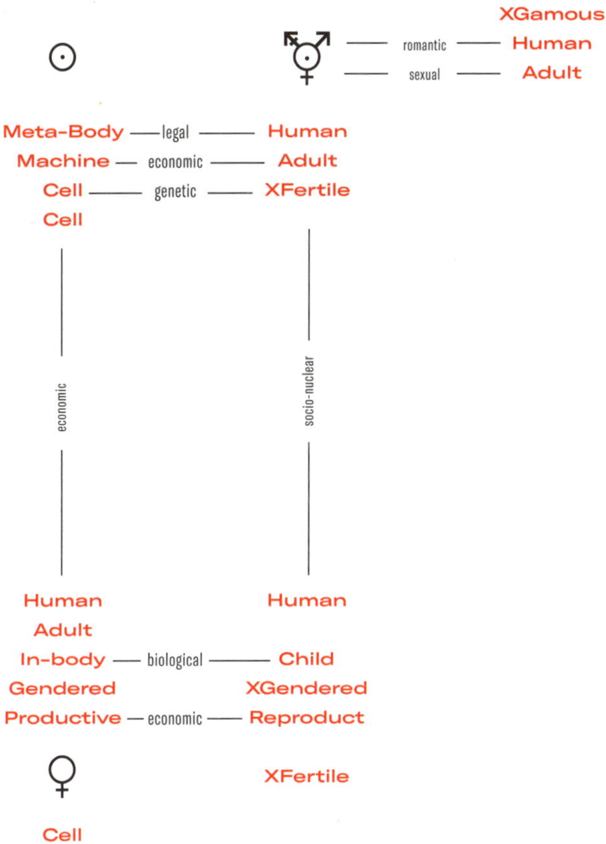

3.

In Repro-Evolution or Reprovolution, as I-as-us call it, a set of other entities enter the diagram's geometry, constructing new and more complex relations. Those relations are brought about by the rupture of reproduction technologies entering the reproductive grid, disrupting and reconnecting biological, genetic, social, and sexual relations. Formerly "biologically fenced" generational layers and geographically distant locales might collapse: a Danish sperm donor "begets" a child in Japan, or a grandmother giving birth to her grandchildren with her daughter's embryo.

In the diagram the vertical lines represent cross-generational connections, while distances of local realties are represented through different symbols for reproductive entities. Also with the introduction of a machine—i.e., a cryofreezer—or the particle of a formerly coherent body—i.e., a stem cell—the repro-architecture no longer has to involve humans.

The external genetic donor can be a human subject that can still be related through their "donation" of the cell. In other cases, they can be still related through relations of sexual and biological reproductivity.

Yet, all relations are still drawn in vertical and horizontal lines in a grid, indicating the unchanged systemic determination of these seemingly new relations for capitalist ReproNormality: they socially, aesthetically, and politically reproduce the family structure instead of dissolving it.

The dotted circle symbolizes a non-gendered, particled entity of reproduction: a stem cell. Such cells are carried by adult, human subjects regardless of their gender identity; they reproduce not because of their biological binary, but are driven by a mechanism to trade and reconfigure DNA. The Reproduct of genders and sexes alike is made "off-body." I-as-us propose that with off-body reproduction, all reproduction has become genderless, as it fragments into microbiological or molecular exchanges of matter and information, in which gendering vectors and at some level sexual differentiation collapses. With each in-vitro fertilization, between twelve and twenty-four stem cells—also called single-celled embryos—are produced. The extracted stem cell—held by the pipette and watched over by the microscope and cared for by synthetic nourishing fluids—is a body-in-difference. It is apparently machinic and driven by information. Even though biological, this particle knows no boundary between the natural, the artificial, the microscopic, and the planetary. As a carrier of information, this cell can be frozen—contrary to the human body—and therefore it's disjointed in time and place. Human Reproduction can happen all over the globe and all over time. We think of it as a Data Body.

ReproTechnoTribal (beta)

Reprovolution — collectively disrupted system determination

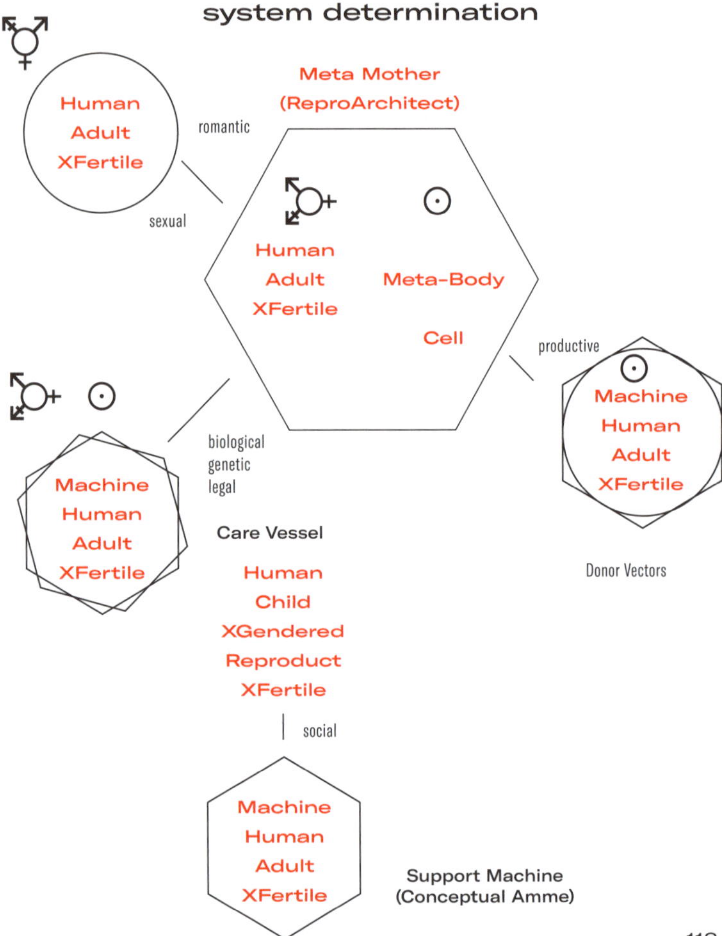

4.

The last diagram is the most speculative, and operates on an assumption that ReproRevolution is not only a feature of financialized and bio-digital capitalism, but that it can be collectively disrupted and appropriated for means it wasn't invented for. Disrupting ReproNormality draws on the idea that technologies of reproduction can be extracted from their current biopolitical systemic determinations. It's the political nexus in which the reproduction of capital and (human) life itself intersect. The relations that unfold from these practices are what I-as-us call the ReproTechnoTribe (beta): a sketch and approximation of what is potentially possible when repro-tech is redirected to diffuse, instead of reaffirm, the family structure as the only legitimate reproduction container.

In the diagram, I-as-us appropriate conceptual personae from heteropatriarchal, bio-digital, capitalist repro-cultures and organize a psycho-realist détournement of their respective functions. The methodology entails assigning different values to certain forms of reproductive labor and redirecting the economies of desire towards alternate purposes—an alternative repro-communal economy of reproducing human life. The diagram creates a reproductive architecture from various mothering personae and identities that are constructed, rather than the concrete forms that we still operate with.

Please do not understand this diagram as a program to initiate a currently functioning Repro-container. This is an example of how various new Repro-personae could possibly come together to form a Reproduct. It asks: What is a mother, if we were to give the term an expanded meaning?

Some of the most important are the MetaMothers. They are ReproArchitects, and can be individuals or groups of people who decide to involve themselves in reproduction. Consequently they can be of any gender determination or self-framing and in any relationship to one another. It doesn't matter for a MetaMother of a ReproTechnoTribe if you're born female, feel male; if you repro-drag or whatever your gender is. I-as-us appropriated this conceptual persona from the term "intending parents," which is an important legal term in the current repro-technology market. Those are the persons that are given the full rights and credits to the child. They are owners and they are—especially in US-American law—the only persons within the reproductive structure that become visible and endowed with parental rights.

Then there are the Mother Vessels that gestate cells and bring them to fruition. While there is a good chance that the gestation of any Reproduct will be automated in the next century, in today's Reprovolution, they become equally part of a reproductive architecture and not excluded from visibility and stakeholdership, like in the current ReproNormality.

Then there are the Donor Mothers, whose role is to publish data in the form of genetic material. I-as-us think of genetic data as a form of commons of the entire species. Communal genetics is essential in new family models, especially because genes are currently treated as proprietary information and are exploited for-profit in sperm and egg banks. From the perspective of a planetary and communal Repro-Architecture, genetic material would be thought of as shareable without loss and therefore would have specific non-proprietary licensing implications. I-as-us would again put forward a reworked concept of the body in Reprovolution and propose an expanded notion of sperm and ovo banks as communal Data Bodies, which are involved in reproducing the species. Data Bodies that we provide in service of expanded family platforms; bodies of information that we collect and retain on one another during our time on earth and use for mutual aid and collective creation; Data Bodies that we publish in the form of cryo-containers.

For the sake of readability, I-as-us have left out the intergenerational fragmentation of time by means of cryo-time that is the consequence of the genetic commons in a repro-architecture. If you would insert time into this diagram, you would have relations that would move beyond biological age: e.g., "I'm 70. I want a younger person to create a ReproTechnoTribe with my genetic material, and I don't live to see it become form." Or you could sow your cells into a cryo-container and contract donor mothers and wet nurses in the far future to raise a Reproduct without the sequence of generations in between you and them. I have called this form "Reptile Reproduction," and I'm developing the next set of diagrams on this basis.

There is also the obvious question: Who finances any singular reproductive structure? A non-nuclear repro-architecture needs Support Mothers or wet nurses who provide funds. They might provide neither time, nor labor, nor data, but will contribute to the Repro-architecture financially in solidarity with reproducing the species in itself, while they are not involved as any other form of mothering.

Molecular Reproduction

I-as-us don't consider of what the diagrams try to sketch out not as an extended family that is connected through different social bonds and social interactions; I-as-us think of the ReproTribe as more of an expanded family as a platform—a platform on which reproductive resources are shared between various people and technologies.

Contrary to the "sharing economy," which will very likely move toward making reproduction a business model in the coming years, I-as-us would envision this platform as a non-biological reproduction cooperative.[5] For this model to be non-nuclear it needs to be an association by a variety of bonds, which I-as-us drew as different lines that are more or less strong. Family as a set of various elements that are connected: atoms of elements such as silicon, oxygen, and carbon form different molecular bonds, thereby producing different formations similar to how we humans see the qualities or properties of a substance instead of its molecular composition.[6] In us-as-our molecular reproduction, various connections might be still classified as social, technological, financial, and even genetic, while the expanded family as a ReproTribe and a platform is functioning more like the chemical periodic system: atomized humans becoming molecular structures in millions of systematic connections. I-as-us would like reproduction to become molecular in the sense that once you're connected, your formation becomes so different in properties and qualities that others can't recognize your repro-structure as an essence. It's the end of the family as a recognizable and essential structure, while human relations and mutual aid to one another is still capable of bringing about diversity and forming a society of justice.

Hyperemotionalization as an expression of crisis

One other potential of the ReproTechnoTribe as an expanded family platform in disrupted Reprovolution is that it can produce chimeras: structural relations of being together that you cannot recognize anymore, that we don't yet have the terms for. Repro-tech exposes the political and even fascist implication of ideology-driven family values that manifest themselves in hyper-emotionalized language. There is no more biological or natural necessity for the family with repro-tech anymore. Technology has pulverized the modern biological basis of these coercive forms. For us-as-me, it has the potential to constitute unreadable connectivities, unreadable bonds, and unreadable formations. There is a potential to create an entire set of relations of unreadability; unreadable to the state and to capital.

What I-as-us did not discuss in detail is a residue of natural human procreation: sex. In the ReproTribe, sexuality and pleasure can entirely vanish from the reproductive model. Of course they will continue to exist, and as a modernist remnant of reproduction they both are still locatable in the diagram. But they are disconnected and externalized from the reproductive vectors. What actually happens in the ReproTechnoTribe is that sexuality is not a part of the reproductive architecture anymore and it will not be an issue that has to be dealt with.

1 Transformella and her SelfSisters are artificial identities assembled and fed since 2010 toward becoming psycho-real alifveForms by J.P. Raether.

2 "I-as-us" is an invented pronoun for an identitarian paradox that claims identity disorder as a productive force, and at the same time represents it as a method in the continuous process of self-identification. It describes the constructed "we" of artificial identities that research, write, and build devices and environments as a psycho-real herd of selves.

3 Ikeality is more commonly seen to refer to the labyrinthine showroom of an IKEA store. In Transformella malor ikeae's cosmology of Reprovolution, however, Ikeality is the core of a rhizomatic system that has rooted through the entire planet, relating each singular and local Ikeality to its same, but different global twin, repeating 433 times. The resulting interconnected and nested array of trypophobic entities is a mad dance of growth and commodity terror, aimed at the bio-digital family for strengthening its immunological resilience against its own dissolution by the forces that sustain it: Uterocapitalist Repro-technology.

4 Data Body is a device used by Transformella malor ikeae and derivatae

for providing data (diagrams, audio, photos, and videos, etc.) to the distributed particles of their associtaed formation of Sisters in the Coming ReproCommunal Tribe.

5 Arguably, the “rent a womb“ internet marketing campaign of the 2010s will morph into a social media driven ReproAirBnB in the next decade. Freelance surrogacy is on the horizon.

6 If you look at silicon, for example, it’s classified as a metal. When it’s in elemental form, it’s very shiny and really looks like a metal. When you expose it to oxygen, it forms thousands of possible molecular bonds and the substance starts to become mineral. Ninety-five percent of Earth’s stone mantle is silicon and oxygen bonded in various formations.

Contagion Propagations

Jonas Staal

A contrast that matters: former US vice president Joe Biden appeals to the public in a pseudo-presidential address in the midst of his 2020 campaign for the Democratic nomination against Bernie Sanders, and calls for bipartisanship in the face of the outbreak, claiming that the "coronavirus does not have a political affiliation." Sanders meanwhile appeals to the public on the same day, but instead criticizes the $1.5 trillion infusion into Wall Street by the Federal Reserve to save private companies, and drives home the added urgency of his key policy proposal, Medicare for All, especially in the midst of an outbreak in which the most vulnerable and precarious among us will be hit hardest.

Biden is wrong, as he has always been. The coronavirus certainly *has* a political affiliation—with the alt-right, big pharma, and the securitization industry, which will make ideological gains and grotesque profits from this crisis. The virus makes visible the ideological framework underlying our political, economic, and social infrastructures—or their ruins after decades of austerity and privatization. A meme circulating on social media in March 2020 shows the image of a virus with the line "Nice country you've got there, would be a shame if it laid bare the cruelty inherent in its very structure." And this is exactly the point: the *material propagation* of the coronavirus makes visible a series of *ideological propagations*, both past and present, with severe consequences.

The question in front of us is: What alternative propagations can withstand the threat not only of the coronavirus, but of the far worse pandemics and system failures we will face in the climate catastrophes of the near future? Asking this also means confronting the difficult question of why the political platform of Bernie Sanders has failed to clench the nomination—especially in a time in which his social policies have broader support and are proven more urgent than ever before.

1. From Covid-19 to the Specter of Eco-Fascism

Let's begin at the beginning. The coronavirus itself is inherently intertwined with global capitalism, which, as urban theorist Mike Davis argues, now appears to be "biologically unsustainable" in the absence of a truly international public health infrastructure.[1] Covid-19 has been replicated through global trade and transport, a network hailed as the best of all possible worlds that again proves to be extremely vulnerable and dependent upon taxpayer money—an infusion meant to keep intact the very system that creates the conditions for these types of global contaminations in the first place. The climate catastrophe, which is enabled by the very same industrialist and extractivist mindset, will only amplify such pandemics in the near future. In the words of The Red Nation, "The crisis has exposed the capitalist system for what it is: anti-life."[2]

Cheers for the reduction of CO_2 emissions resulting from the pandemic—as if this was some global exercise in degrowth—ring hollow in the context of a death toll largely consisting of people who were already extremely vulnerable, either due to structural racial oppression, preexisting illnesses, old age, homelessness, incarceration, undernourishment, or war. The economic damage caused by the pandemic has been disproportionately transferred to the working and precarious classes, who simultaneously have to pay up to save private corporations and banks through tax infusions. The ruling classes have their private clinics, respiratory support systems, and luxury bunkers—so the joy expressed when Jair Bolsonaro was proven to be infected or the ongoing speculation about Donald Trump's illness will be short lived. They were never going to suffer from this the same way we were anyway. Even worse is the cynical ageist embrace of the virus as a way to rid the welfare state of elderly people, a dark foreshadowing of the genocidal engineering strategies which we will hear more of as the eco-fascist movement comes to the fore.

All of this exemplifies a preexisting mentality: every day, tens of thousands of people die because of poverty, exploitation, and warfare. People who are now most acutely confronted with this virus are those for whom measures such as "social distancing," regular handwashing with water and soap, and working at home sound absolutely absurd. Consider just that 25 percent of the world population already lacks access to adequate sanitation.[3] According to Noam Chomsky and Edward S. Herman, such people fall into the category of those who, in the eyes of the imperialists, are to be considered "unworthy victims," compared to their own "worthy victims."[4] The latter are those who, in Judith Butler's words, are regarded as human enough by ruling elites to be "grievable" in the first place.[5] In the context of a pandemic, the Global North is no longer able to fully externalize the unworthy victims offshore—the unworthy ones now also come to include the elderly, the unemployed, and those with preexisting conditions within our borders. They were always less valued than the white and able-bodied, but are now reduced to collateral damage in the fight to protect "worthy citizens" from becoming worthy victims.

At this point, we have not even addressed the racialization of the coronavirus, the alt-right contagion that spread even faster than the virus itself. Hate crimes against people of Asian descent, the equation of bodies of color with disease—this all follows the textbook propaganda strategy of Fritz Hippler's Nazi faux-documentary *Der ewige Jude* (The Eternal Jew, 1940), in which rats and other vermin were used to allegorize Jews in Europe. Alt-right ideologue and filmmaker Steve Bannon was quick to embrace and propagate the narrative that the coronavirus is actually a bioweapon manufactured in a secret Chinese lab, which serves to deepen his conspiracy that the People's Republic of China is at the center of a new axis of evil, while adding legitimacy to Trump's border wall, as the virus and the migrant become conflated into one big threat aimed at infecting the sovereign body of the United States. It did not take long for this narrative to contaminate Trump's daily hate speech briefings, in which the coronavirus was rebranded as the "Chinese Virus." In India, Prime Minister Narendra Modi's Bharatiya Janata Party claims a direct relation between Muslims and the coronavirus, which has led to an outbreak of targeted violence. Hungary's far-right president, Viktor Orbán, claimed a direct link between the coronavirus and the threat of "illegal" migration and has, in the meantime, suspended parliament altogether.

The racialization of the coronavirus obviously follows from conditions of the culture wars that precede the pandemic, in which one front has been drawn by ultranationalist and hard right parties and another by the global capitalist elite. Between the capitalists attempting to maintain hegemony and the nationalists seeking to racialize the virus, the culture wars give us *eco-fascism* as the ideological paradigm of the world we face after this pandemic—a world in which climate catastrophe will inevitably generate far more of these global viruses in the near future.[6] It is via eco-fascism that the fatal myth of overpopulation is spreading even faster in the context of the present crisis. The capitalist class has never shown any hesitancy in declaring vast parts of the population irrelevant to work or consumption, and white nationalists have long been on the lookout for conditions in which to turn their genocidal fantasies into reality.

But the eco-fascist myth risks contaminating progressive discourse just the same. Think of the Michael Moore-produced film *Planet of the Humans* (2019), directed by his long-term collaborator Jeff Gibbs, launched online in the midst of the coronavirus outbreak. The film claims to advance a legitimate critique of "green capitalism," but instead uses dated research and misplaced image sources to argue that it requires more fossil fuel to produce solar and wind powered energy resources than they can ever hope to generate—a narrative that was quickly embraced by the alt-right media outlet Breitbart News. Instead, Gibbs argues, we have to confront the issue of overpopulation, because "our human presence is already far beyond sustainability" and "it's not the carbon dioxide molecule destroying the planet, it's us."[7] But population growth in the Global North is at an all-time low, while energy consumption is unsustainably high, which then automatically leads to pointing the finger at the higher population growth in the Global South, whose consumption rate is infinitely lower. The racialized myth of overpopulation bypasses the fact that it is not human population but the global capitalist system that is ecologically unsustainable, enabling the murderous eugenics that inform eco-fascism instead. As researcher Sherronda J. Brown writes:

> [W]e have to understand that institutional and corporate disregard for the planet cannot be divorced from disregard for marginalized beings from those same destructive systems. Know that when you post and share variations of "humans are the virus" online, you are parroting the rhetoric of white supremacists. Instead of doing that, I encourage you to remind others and yourselves of the capitalist, corporate, colonialist, and imperialist failings of a deeply unequal world.[8]

What we witness in the pandemic is an accelerated propagation of ideological forms inherent to the "deeply unequal world" that Brown describes, which in the process lay the groundwork for an eco-fascist future. But these narratives can also be traced to an imaginary of a world that is beyond communal governance, and which can only be taken "back into control"—to paraphrase the ultranationalist Brexiteer slogan—through brutal engineering strategies.

2. The Ungovernable World

Various Hollywood pandemic movies have laid the groundwork for the successful racialization of the pandemic. Whether it is the Motaba virus modeled after Ebola in *Outbreak* (1995), or the MEV-1 virus modeled after SARS in *Contagion* (2011), the virus always originates in a "foreign" body. For US empire, all that is foreign is to be both feared *and* extracted, whether from Zaire or Hong Kong. In *World War Z* (2013), the most telling scene shows the arrival of survivors of a zombie plague in Israel, whose US-subsidized weapons and surveillance industry have made it the rare world actor capable of withstanding the contagion (a scenario that obviously aims to legitimize the maintenance of the occupation of Palestine and its foreign backing in the present). In the film, it is the high-pitched singing of Arab refugees who had been benevolently taken in by their occupier that finally triggers the hordes of zombies to overtake the Israeli fortress, despite all precautions, proposing the deeply offensive and revisionist narrative that it is essentially Israeli *altruism* that forms its true vulnerability.[9] Such a worldview sees a superior military-industrial complex as mandatory to secure the survival of worthy citizens, an idea that goes hand-in-hand with the unequivocal framing of Palestinians as an unworthy zombie race beyond redemption.

Such pandemic cinema has further engrained in us certain behavioral responses to disaster. Another zombie-type virus in *28 Weeks Later* (2002) renders survivors more dangerous to one another than the zombies are (from "humans are the virus" to "humans are the zombies," although *some* humans are always more zombie than others). Here, or in the more allegorical infertility epidemic in *Children of Men* (2006), we the precariat are expected to largely fend for ourselves, hoard food, medicine, and weapons, and trust governing elites to impose brutal securitization measurements upon us, praying that we are exempted from their worst consequences, while they themselves save cultural treasures to gaze upon in their securitized private bunkers. These narratives suppose the antiquated social psychology of Gustave Le Bon's *The Crowd: A Study of the Popular Mind* (1895). Le Bon's concept of the crowd would influence the widely used notion of the "herd," which he describes as an "unstable flock"[10] consisting of a "swarm of isolated individuals," so easily manipulated as to be barbaric.[11] It is not difficult to see the parallel between these popular imaginaries and the framing of humans as the virus. While it is global capitalism that is biologically unsustainable, here the idea is that it is "human nature" itself that is laying ruin to the earth and other life sustaining structures, and that this is a truth revealed only to its full extent in times of crisis, when worthy humans must face the unworthy zombies that used to be tolerated in their midst.

This reactionary mindset that takes (particular) humans as a barbarous herd has been instilled in governing elites through decades of war gaming, developed by the likes of the RAND Corporation. Think of the *Atlantic Storm* game, staged by the Center for Biosecurity at the University of Pittsburgh Medical Center in 2005 as a ministerial tabletop exercise.[12] The script starts with a fictional multination summit in Washington, DC, when reports suddenly come in that a massive terrorist attack in Europe is taking place in the form of a rapidly spreading smallpox virus.[13] Senior government leaders played the role of heads of state assembled at the summit, with Madeleine Albright acting as the US president.[14] As news of casualties rolls in, the message of the game scenario is clear: the combination of disease and terrorism poses a threat greater than all the wars of the past century combined, cultivating a scenario in which only the most drastic responses are imaginable—militarization of public health infrastructures, extreme securitization, a disregard for any existing laws, and unlimited patriotism and nationalism to protect at least part of the population. In other words, from the perspective of *Atlantic Storm*, the world is no longer governable through common means—a situation familiar to the Italian government, which at the height of its crisis was refused help of medical supplies from Germany: all can ungovern for themselves. With these cultural artifacts we are thus scripted into the idea that it is scarcity—whether the lack of toilet paper and intensive care equipment, or worse, massive crop failure and the disappearance of inhabitable land—that determines how we respond to others in order to ensure some form of survival. Suddenly, democratic governance, human rights, and privacy are revealed as the luxuries that they supposedly always were, and elite engineering—such as population control—remains the only viable option.

So far, governments in the Global North affected by the virus have largely privileged the continuity of economic activity and the healthy pulse of the Dow Jones rather than the healthy pulse of the actual living and breathing members of their populations—the United Kingdom's initial strategy of "herd immunity" being the most cynical, brutally weighing the collateral damage of its own seemingly disposable population against the "greater good" of market stability. This strategy was consequently adopted as the main approach of the Dutch government, who euphemistically reframed it as an "intelligent lock-down." The seeds of an engineering mentality are clearly planted, and as governments increasingly realize that an on-and-off series of lockdowns is the only scenario for the next year at least, we need to be prepared for the *Atlantic Storm* mindset to come further into play, with the help of the security industry, for which a pandemic is nothing but the next market opportunity. And while the current coronavirus pandemic is ultimately containable, we need to understand we are seeing a dangerous blueprint emerging as the specter of eco-fascism rises to meet the inevitable climate crises of new pandemics, food scarcity, and millions of refugees yet to come.

3. Red Virus International

The conditions emerging from the pandemic enable different pathways forward: they can become the basis for the propagation of "shock doctrine" austerity, racism, and mass securitization, or for the propagation of radical new forms of socialization and collective care. In the words of Naomi Klein:

> If there's one thing history teaches us it's that moments of shock are profoundly volatile. We either lose a whole lot of ground, get fleeced by elites, and pay the price for decades, or we win progressive victories that seemed impossible just a few weeks earlier. This is no time to lose our nerve. The future will be determined by whoever is willing to fight harder for the ideas they have lying around.[15]

In José Saramago's novel *Blindness* (1998), a small group of quarantined people try to survive an epidemic of blindness in an unspecified country. In the story, the narrative of the securitization of the ungovernable world is central. But in Saramago's subsequent novel, *Seeing* (2004), the epidemic is no longer biological but *social*: at election time, people vote for nobody, leaving the ballot blank instead. No matter what anti-terrorist policies the government of the same unspecified country impose to deter this "subversive" behavior, people leave the ballot blank in higher and higher numbers. As punishment, the government decides to abandon its people, and the people in turn respond by organizing collective health care and food distribution themselves.

For a long time, I wrongfully believed that *Seeing* was a manifesto for leaving the ballot blank. Later on, I realized it is a literary manifesto for our ability to respond *differently* and *transformatively* to the crises that the regimes under which we live impose upon us. In the US, the Democratic Party establishment did everything in its power to frame a vote for Sanders as a blank vote, because he supposedly never got anything done as a senator and would never get anything done as president. Better to vote for Biden, they say, and join those who maintain the status quo responsible for the crises of the present, in which we are left to praying to be recognized as worthy citizens entitled to a right of survival. But this is not a world worth propagating.

Instead, from Italy to Iran, streets have been filled with chants of solidarity from balcony to balcony. Autonomist groups have quickly organized the necessary structures of life support for those who were already by and large abandoned as worthy citizens. Comrades—when they are fortunate enough to do so—practice social distancing to be nearer to one another, as they further socialize goods and digital means of communication to enable alternative modes of gathering and assembly. Healthcare workers share their own health with those affected. Unions are at the doors of parliament demanding compensation for the precarious classes, and cultural workers popularize the demand "Close everything, pay everyone!"[16] Activists and social workers demand the immediate evacuation of refugee camps in Greece and of ICE detention centers in the US. Spain's first left government since the end of fascism has instantly taken control over private health infrastructures—and now it's up to us to make sure they never privatize it back again. The Black Lives Matter movement has taken hold worldwide, making visible the brutal additional toll of the pandemic to the already structural murder of Black people everywhere, and enforcing radical transformation of the security apparatus through the demand "Defund the Police." As political theorist Jodi Dean noted, in the early weeks following the pandemic breakout:

> The truth of capitalism presents itself in all its naked horror in a crisis. Everyone hates the hoarders and profiteers. We appreciate purchase limits, laws against price gouging. We all recognize that healthcare is too important to be left to the market. As the cruelty of the market appears without its ideological sheen, more and more people realize the necessity—for the good of all—of free medical care, of paid medical leave, of a social safety net. Everyone's a socialist now (whether they have recognized it or not).[17]

Here we see the possibility of propagating a different contamination; not a biological virus, but a virus of egalitarian ideas. A red virus, that has turned policies such as universal healthcare, fair pay for care workers and cleaners, and basic income into newly mainstream demands. But if the red virus has been successful in changing the discourse surrounding our commons and in forming a front against the ungovernable world and the specter of eco-fascism, it has not yet insured a structural stake in new emancipatory forms of governance. In other words, if we can't have Sanders now, then when?

The propagation of the red virus opens a trajectory in which we can engage this pandemic transformatively, but in doing so, we cannot ignore the recent past. Countries where emancipatory politics succeeded not only in the street, but in in gaining a stake in institutional governance as well—such as Spain—have the relative means to enable this moment of transformation, as the Podemos coalition has done not only by temporarily nationalizing private health care but also by trying to implement a universal basic income on a longer term basis. Compare that to Greece, where the conservative-right New Democracy party has succeeded the social democratic Syriza party, and its government rents ICU beds from private clinics to meet demand. In other words, the coronavirus pandemic shows that in order to script the crisis away from disaster capitalism into a transformative politics, it is crucial to lay an emancipatory claim on governing institutions—even if the full-scale demand is the total remaking of those institutions all together.

We cannot ignore the waning influence of emancipatory political parties and unions when it comes to building infrastructures that can channel the energies of politicized crowds—such as those the red virus propagates into being—into organized and disciplined bodies of change. In Dean's words, "commonality arises not out of identity, not out of who one is, but out of what is being done—fighting, circulating, studying, traveling, or being part of the same apparatus."[18] The Sanders campaign has been one of exceptional organizational skill, but the longer ruling neoliberal norm of the Democratic Party makes it hard for supporters of his ideas to believe they are materially realizable in the present, and the face of his platforms leadership is still far from acquiring the "leaderful" form of Black Lives Matter.[19] Whereas Biden can promise a return to the normal of the neoliberal Barack Obama era, Sanders must reach back as far as the New Deal era to make the case that his ideas of the future build on real gains of the past. And even this, as proponent of the Green New Deal Alexandria Ocasio-Cortez highlighted, is deeply problematic because: "We act as though the New Deal wasn't racist. The New Deal was an incredibly economically racist policy that drew literal red lines around Black and Brown communities. And basically it invested in white America, and . . . allowed white Americans to have access to home loans that Black and Brown Americans did not have access to, giving them the largest form of intergenerational wealth, which is real estate."[20] Ocasio-Cortez stresses the leaderful emphasis as a counterpoint, by arguing that "this is why the intersectional frontline community aspect of the Green New Deal is so important, because it allows indigenous communities to lead, and for Black and Brown communities to have a certain self-determination that has not existed in public policy."[21] Instead of making an imagined past "great again," this organizational endeavor thus aims to be transformative rather than nostalgic.

In the current pandemic, policies of social distancing and self-quarantine seem to be opposite to the physical closeness historically required for shaping the commonalities Dean references to build the popular power needed to enforce transformative change. But there is also an opportunity to build nearness not through the proximity of our bodies, but through the infrastructures that connect and sustain us. The red virus produces unexpected allies—even pop star Britney Spears called for a general strike and a redistribution of wealth at the height of the pandemic, and was subsequently rebranded "Comrade Britney." But, as Dean argues, "comradeship is a disciplining relation," and thus supposes the need to create and maintain an infrastructure that sustains common struggle and enables the necessary power to turn egalitarian imaginaries into egalitarian realities.[22]

The point is, organizational closeness goes beyond proximity. There was closeness achieved through the disciplinary relation of comradeship in the former Comintern, but this ideological intimacy is one structured by egalitarian ideas and shared work—even when the bodies sharing these ideas and work are far apart from one another—resulting in the profound experience of becoming something more by being on the same side, together in the fight to collectively bring a new world into being. The necessity to critique the Comintern, particularly after its Stalinist turn, does nothing to alter the loss of a transnational body of comradely organization, particularly in a moment like the one we are facing now. The Green New Deal is one of the rare viable policy proposals of our time to ensure some form of meaningful common survival—human, non-human, and more-than-human alike—but it needs now to be pressed upon neoliberal and increasingly far-right regimes who, if they adopt any of its plans at all, will do so from their desire to either maintain the capitalist paradigm under a green guise or impose eco-fascist eugenics, or a combination of the two. That the pandemic moment coincides with the declaration of a new Progressive International, initiated by the Democracy in Europe Movement 2025 (DiEM25) and the Sanders Institute, is crucial, but it will only succeed if the red virus does not merely propagate the desire for new egalitarian imaginaries, but also the organizational willingness to bring them into being.

In this light, the role of emancipatory culture is vital. The commonized world still needs art and literature, poetry and film, to enable narratives in which crisis does not reduce us into hoarders and preppers, but creates new communal frameworks, symbols, and shared powers instead. That also means that this culture cannot be created as a "swarm of isolated individuals," as Le Bon called us, but as comrades structured organizationally in a twenty-first century International. For the elites, this might be an ungovernable world. But we still have many worlds to propagate, in which to live and love in comradely care.

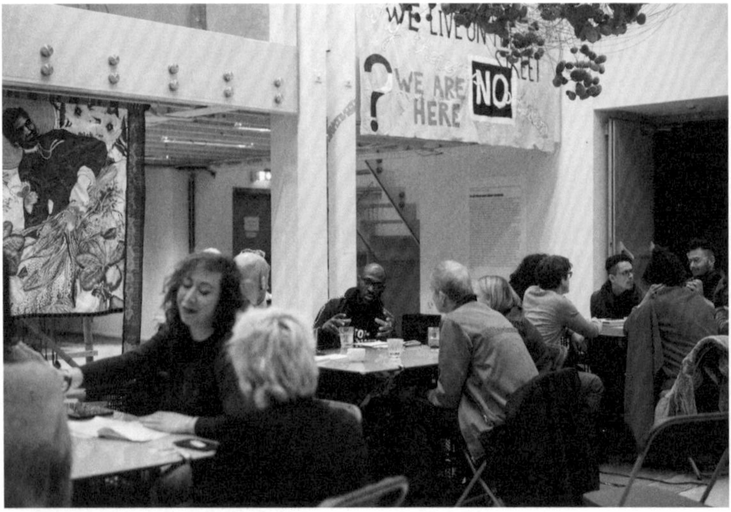

Working groups at Jonas Staal's *Organizational Art Training* in the framework of *Propositions #9: Deserting from the Culture Wars*, BAK, basis voor actuele kunst, Utrecht, 13 November 2019, photo: Tom Janssen

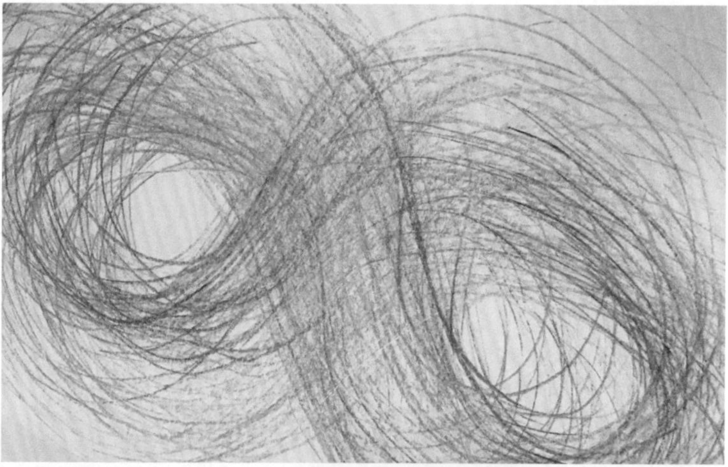

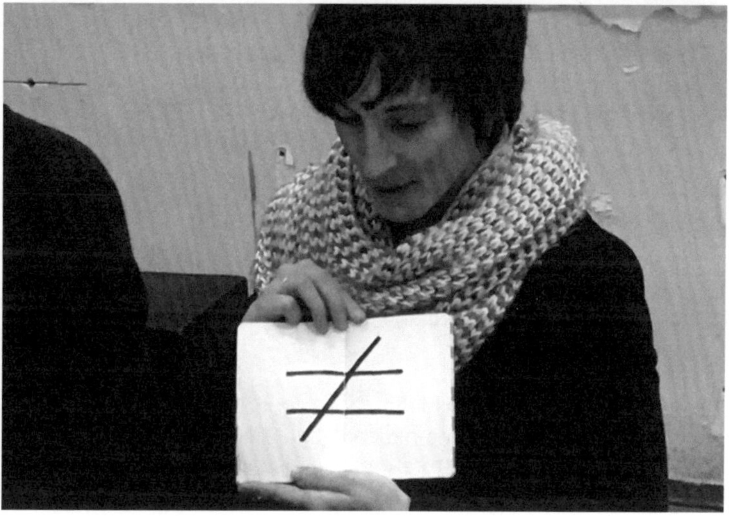

Logos of the artist organizations Time Travelers' Alliance (top) and Conspiracy of Unequals (bottom), originated at Jonas Staal's *Organizational Art Training* in the framework of *Propositions #9: Deserting from the Culture Wars*, BAK, basis voor actuele kunst, Utrecht, 13 November 2019, photo: Sven Lütticken

Post Scriptum: Organizational Art Training Manual

How do we organize in, with, and through art? How to elaborate concrete tactics to propagate for and to contribute to the movements that are engaged in emancipatory practices of world-making? What is the role of art and artistic competence in contributing to the imaginary of new alternative transnational infrastructure of self-governance and collective care? On request of the editors of this reader, what follows is a possible contribution to the real time propagation of the red virus and the egalitarian life-forms it makes possible: a training manual for organizational art, developed before the coronavirus pandemic and offered here for adoption and adaptation.

What I term "organizational art" is practiced through the model of the artist organization—political parties, campaigns, laboratories, social platforms, and schools—conceived both as political organizations *and* as artworks. In 2015, the Artist Organizations International at the Hebbel am Ufer Theater in Berlin—which I co-organized with Joanna Warsza and Florian Malzacher—brought together over 20 of such organizations. The twenty-first century has seen a substantial rise in organizational art, developed by artists who aim to work in direct relation to popular movements and transform their collective imaginaries into durational infrastructural morphologies.[23]

Think, for example, of Tania Bruguera's artist organization Immigrant Movement International (IMI, 2010–2015), which operated from a storefront in a former beauty salon in Queens, NY, where Bruguera and her collaborators organized English lessons, provided legal support for immigrants, established cultural workshops for children, and collectively authored the *International Migrant Manifesto* (2011).[24] This modest community center operated as a practical space of empowerment, while at the same time announcing itself as the first building block of a radically new transnational organization declaring the immigrant as a new "global citizen."[25] In this planetary détournement, it would not be the migrant that has to adapt to the logics of the state, but the state that must transform to meet the shared reality of being-migrant. Another example would be Ahmet Öğüt's The Silent University (SU, 2012–ongoing), an alternative school that operates through art institutions and universities that provides a teaching platform to immigrants with an academic background who are unrecognized for their competences in their country of arrival. As such, SU "un-silences" knowledge, and since its founding, has been active in London, Stockholm, Hamburg, Ruhr, Amman, and Athens. Similar to IMI, SU operates somewhere between the real and the possible. It has been modestly successful in providing academic work for its members but is unambiguous in its near-utopian ambition to reject traditional currencies, overthrow pedagogical hierarchies, demand equality of all languages, and recognize silence as an alternative form of knowledge transfer.[26]

The rise of global authoritarianism, structural racism, precarity, and climate collapse means that the demand for a new imaginary of transnational infrastructure is the only reasonable act to guarantee a form of meaningful earthly survival. But this will require insistence on translating artistic imaginaries into political realities in order to avoid this new infrastructural organizational art mappings from becoming the symbol of its own impotence. In that sense, the artist organization has the obligation to measure its imagination in relation to its real-time capacity to ensure durational political transformation.

The diverse methodology of organizational art practice, operating between the real and the possible, provides crucial means of mobilizing the popular imaginary. As artistic work in political parties and activist platforms is often forced to respond within the conditions and urgencies produced by the order that they themselves wish to abolish, organizational art can contribute to demanding not just what is possible within the systems that present themselves as given but for the fundamental reorganizations of these very systems. In other words, organizational art emphasizes the demand for the impossible as the only realistic thing to do—and working for liberation from the supposedly natural order as the way to unleash the collective desire to *demand more*.

This does not mean to deny the constraints of day-to-day responses to immediate urgencies, but rather to insist simultaneously on a relentless demand for the alternative horizon we actually wish to achieve. It is crucial to respond in the here and now when it comes to supporting refugees, ensuring democratic socialist voter turnout, or resisting ultranationalist parties and governments, but it is just as urgent to insist on a profound transformation of the structures of governance toward those that would recognize migrants as the norm and the state as the exception, or to demand new transnational models of emancipatory governance in which the very notion of nationalism as a point of reference is annihilated all together. The realistic and the possible do not negate one another but enable each other.

The following is a manual for an organizational art training that requires at least four to five hours, to which the preceding text can serve as an introduction through a collective reading group. Obviously, many artist organizations were developed over several years and cannot be replicated in the short time frame of the training. Therefore, it is first and foremost a training in a *methodology* that can be applied in real time if the participants wish to dedicate themselves to further organizing work. But even if this is not the case, the below guidelines stand as an imaginative exercise that draws from artistic, campaigning, and activist practices.

The organizational art training can be practiced with groups ranging from 15 to 50 people, depending on the available time. Ideally, the participants differ in discipline, mixing together artists, designers, architects, filmmakers, students, activists, and organizers. After the introductory reading, ask the group to divide themselves into subgroups of a minimum of 5 and a maximum of 8 members, based on *the participants they know the least*. Avoid preexisting organizational bonds or familiarity with one another as far as possible. Ask participants to maintain diversity in each subgroup; avoid, for example, all-male subgroups. And maintain an important rule: the amount of time one member talks in a subgroup should be the same amount that each other member of a subgroup speaks as well. Make space for those who feel less comfortable expressing themselves; don't speak for them.

The subgroups will each be working through four phases: *narrative*, *infrastructure*, *morphology*, and *(re)presentation*. Each of these phases needs a minimum of 45 minutes before the next one is introduced but can also take a day each—again, depending on available time. These four phases are derived from the methodology of existing artist organizations. In considering IMI, for example, the *narrative* is the proposition of the immigrant as the global citizen, the *infrastructure* is the former beauty salon turned campaign headquarters, the *morphology* manifests as a near-utopian transnational political campaign, and the model of *(re)presentation* takes the form of collective workshops, public actions, and collectively written manifestos.

NARRATIVE

I. Identify a common interest.

Participants in each subgroup have different backgrounds and are implicated in and by different forms of struggles. Share concerns and seek, despite these differences, a social issue that all consider urgent.

II. Identify a common objective for change.

Now that a common concern is identified, what desired change is shared across the group? Do not feel restrained by existing oppositions between "problem" and "solution": share genuinely unrestrained desires for the kind of transformation you wish to see with regards to your commonly identified social issue/struggle.

III. Identify a common name that embodies the desired change.

Decide on a working name for your group, one that embodies the common objective of change you have identified. For now, this is a working name that can change through the next phases of the training.

INFRASTRUCTURE

I. Identify the infrastructure needed to bring about the desired change.

Does your desired change demand a school, a political party, a union, a media station? Or is there no preexisting infrastructure you can think of, and does your common demand therefore require a desire for a completely new organizational form of its own?

II. Identify how you can contribute to, access, hijack, or claim an infrastructure.

Are there already organizational forms that reflect your desired change? In this case, think of how you could contribute to them, either as a member or by hijacking, repurposing, or claiming the infrastructure as your own. If there is no existing model that reflects your desired change, think of how you could either transform an existing one or conceptualize the new infrastructural form your common demand needs to manifest in the world.

III. Identify the minimum and maximum demands for the desired change your infrastructure can bring about.

Artist organizations operate between the real and the possible. What is the minimum concrete result you wish to bring about, and what is the maximum? Make sure the maximum is actually a maximum: our manifold crises are the result of what our supposed leaders consider "reasonable," but their reason is our disaster. Be relentless in thinking of the worlds your infrastructure can world.

MORPHOLOGY

I. Identify how your common objective for change translates to common symbols.

What image is evoked by the common name and infrastructure that you have identified? What signs and forms can communicate in an affective way to a public not yet familiar with your organizational art form in the making? Listen carefully to each other's interpretations: what is a common symbol for one person in your group that can be read as exclusionary by another.

II. Identify different applications of your common symbol that fit your objective of desired change.

Is the symbol applied in a traditional way (as a poster, meme, button, shirt) or can it take alternative forms (as public interventions and performative actions), or both?

III. Identify the means to make visible—communicate—your common symbol in the public realm.

In which context do you imagine your common symbol to appear, and how does this context relate to the constituents with the most interest in the change you aim to bring about? Try to think of the way you bring your symbol into the public realm as a first step in pre-enacting the alternative worldview you are trying to bring about.

(RE)PRESENTATION

I. Prepare to introduce your narrative, infrastructure, and morphology as a representative of your artist organization to the other groups.

Avoid merely "briefing" others on your group discussions, try to fully identify with the artist organization you conceptualized and embody the idea that you are its members, its representatives, tasked with convincing, recruiting, and mobilizing supporters.

II. Consider the embodied form of representation (e.g., single representative, co-chair, leaderful).

How do the values of your organization translate to its representation? Did you choose a form with a clear hierarchy, and does it make sense to have only a single representative? Is your organization leaderless, or structured on collective practices and would a co-chair or a collective leaderful presentation be more accurate?

III. Consider the means of representation (e.g., spoken word, performance, printed material, common action).

Think of how the representation of your artist organization links to your common objective of change. Is a public statement most applicable? Or should you be physically absent, letting visual or written components represent your organization for you? Is your strategy of mobilization performative in nature, and do you demand the participation of your public? Should it take place where the training was held, or can you take your public to another location related to your objectives?

In closing, return to your subgroups and ask one another if you would be willing to actually pursue bringing into being the artist organization you have conceptualized. If not, share why, since this tells you something of the difficulties and challenges in organizing work. If the answer is yes, do not hesitate: the world will not organize for us, we can only organize it collectively ourselves.

This essay contains revised and expanded segments of "Coronavirus Propagations" published in *e-flux conversations* (17 March 2020) and "Organizational Art" in Jonas Staal, *Propaganda Art in the 21st Century* (Cambridge, MA: MIT Press, 2019). The "Organizational Art Training Manual" is based on three consecutive organizational art trainings held by Staal at ViZ Laboratory for Visual Culture, Athens (2 November 2019); BAK, basis voor actuele kunst, Utrecht, in the context of *Propositions #9: Deserting from the Culture Wars*, curated by Sven Lütticken as part of *Trainings for the Not-Yet* co-convened by Jeanne van Heeswijk and BAK (13 November 2019); and INSTAR Hannah Arendt Institute for Artivism in Havana (24 December 2019).

1 Mike Davis, "C'est la Lutte Finale," *Progressive International: Blueprint*, 30 April 2020, https://progressive.international/blueprint/34da398a-af05-43bb-9778-c27023932630-la-lutte-finale/en.

2 Editorial Council, "The COVID-19 Pandemic: Capitalism in Crisis," *The Red Nation*, 16 March 2020, https://therednation.org/2020/03/16/the-covid-19-pandemic-capitalism-in-crisis/.

3 CDC Centers for Disease Control and Prevention, "Global WASH Fast Facts," https://www.cdc.gov/healthywater/global/wash_statistics.html.

4 Noam Chomsky and Edward S. Herman, *Manufacturing Consent* (New York: Pantheon Books, 1988), p. 39.

5 See Judith Butler, *Precarious Life* (London: Verso Books, 2004).

6 Naomi Klein, *On Fire: (The Burning) Case for a Green New Deal* (London: Penguin Random House UK, 2019), pp. 40–49.

7 Quoted from Jeff Gibbs, dir., *Planet of the Humans* (2019).

8 Sherronda J. Brown, "Humans Are Not the Virus: Don't Be an Eco-fascist," *Wear Your Voice*, 27 March 2020, https://wearyourvoicemag.com/humans-are-not-the-virus-eco-fascist/.

9 Matt Vornell, "Where the Z Stands for Zionism," *Al Jazeera*, 17 July 2013, https://www.aljazeera.com/indepth/opinion/2013/07/201371183655144583.html.

10 Gustave Le Bon, *The Crowd: A Study of the Popular Mind* (New York: Macmillan, 1896), p. 219.

11 Ibid., p. 229.

12 "Atlantic Storm," Center for Biosecurity at the University of Pittsburgh Medical Center, 2005, https://www.centerforhealthsecurity.org/our-work/

events-archive/2005_atlantic_storm/flash/index.html.

13 Joseph Masco, *The Theater of Operations: National Security Affect from the Cold War to the War on Terror* (Durham, NC: Duke University Press, 2014), p. 173.

14 Bradley T. Smith et al., "Navigating the Storm: Report and Recommendations from the Atlantic Storm Exercise," *Biosecurity and Bioterrorism: Biodefense Strategy, Practice, and Science* 3, no. 3 (2005), p. 258.

15 Naomi Klein, "Coronavirus Capitalism – and how to beat it," *The Intercept*, 16 March 2020, https://theintercept.com/2020/03/16/coronavirus-capitalism/.

16 "Museums, Galleries, Art Fairs, Art Centers, Universities, Theaters, Festivals … Cancel Everything, Pay Everyone!," *Documentations*, 14 March 2020, https://documentations.art/Cancel-everything-pay-everyone.

17 Jodi Dean, "So amazing (but not really) how the truth of capitalism presents itself in all its naked horror in a crisis," Facebook, 14 March 2020, https://www.facebook.com/jodi.dean3/posts/10157862284914277.

18 Jodi Dean, *Comrade: An Essay On Political Belonging* (London: Verso Books, 2019), p. 79.

19 As KUCHENGA, writer and representative of Black Lives Matter UK, explains: "In actual fact, we need to foster the leadership skills of everyone. And I found that to be really enriching in working with Black Lives Matter, because all of our voices are equal. It's something that endues everyone with confidence. And it's really useful, because you're not so easily picked off," *Propositions #2: Assemblisms*, panel "After the Assembly" with Havin Güneşer, KUCHENGA, Kate Shea Baird, and Birgitta Jónsdóttir, BAK, basis voor actuele kunst, Utrecht, 25 November 2017, https://www.youtube.com/watch?v=CkTV60XZju4.

20 See conversation between Alexandria Ocasio-Cortez and Briahna Gray, South by Southwest Festival, Austin, 10 March 2019, https://www.youtube.com/watch?v=JU-SE5eNt04.

21 Ibid.

22 Jodi Dean, *Comrade: An Essay On Political Belonging* (London: Verso Books, 2019), p. 86.

23 See Ekaterina Degot, "The Artist as Director: 'Artist Organisations International' and Its Contradictions," *Afterall: A Journal of Art, Context, and Enquiry*, no. 40 (Autumn/Winter 2015), pp. 20–27.
Whereas the term *morphology* today has significance in domains as varied

as linguistics, biology, and mathematics, Johann Wolfgang von Goethe is considered to have defined the term in relation to the study of plants, explaining it as "the science of form [*Gestalt*], formation [*Bildung*], and transformation [*Umbildung*] of organic bodies." See Johannes Grave, "Ideal and History: Johann Wolfgang Goethe's Collection of Prints and Drawings," *Artibus et Historiae*, vol. 27, no. 53 (2006), p. 183.

24 Tania Bruguera et al., "Migrant Manifesto," *Immigrant Movement International*, November 2011, http://immigrant-movement.us/wp-content/uploads/2011/12/IM-International-Migrant-Manifesto2.pdf.

25 Ibid.

26 Florian Malzacher, Ahmet Öğüt, and Pelin Tan, eds., *The Silent University: Towards a Transversal Pedagogy* (Berlin: Sternberg Press, 2016), pp. 68–71.

The Radical Flu: A Collective Work Document Toward a Performance

Rose Hammer

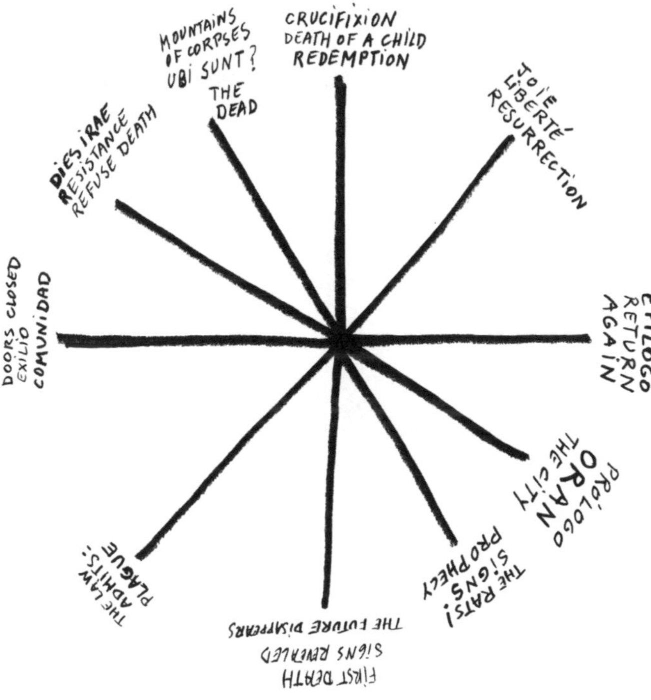

Rose Hammer is an artistic persona consisting of 20 artists that was created as a response to an invitation from osloBIENNALEN First Edition (2019–2024) to create a work in public space. Rose Hammer aims to escape the logic of the individual artist, becoming instead a transnational, transgenerational, and transdisciplinary persona. Rose Hammer carefully considers relatively unknown stories at the origin of widespread conceptions of identity, nationality, and history, in order to construct counternarratives that follow the rules of Brechtian agitprop: with explicit, clearly formulated political positions, non-hierarchical dynamics, and a reductio ad absurdum *of notions such as professionalism, virtuosity, and entertainment.*

Rose Hammer's productions are always site- and context specific; therefore, Rose Hammer responded to osloBIENNALEN's invitation with the work National Episodes, *examining pivotal moments of Norwegian history. In this document, written in February 2020, Rose Hammer collectively constructs their new* National Episode, *based on* The Plague *by Albert Camus (1948) and the opera of the same name by Roberto Gerhard (1963).*

In September 2019, the collective started work on the new episode using working titles such as "The Plague," "The Radical Flu," and "Pharmakos." Reality interrupted this process in a brutal manner with the coronavirus pandemic. Rose Hammer is now working in two temporalities: the period of 1918—which saw the Spanish flu, Socialist revolution, and the rise of feminism—and the present emergency. In this regard, Rose Hammer holds as a model the introductory words in Lars von Trier's 1987 film Epidemic*:*

> A coincidence due to fate can be so sinister and fantastic in character that one is tempted to

draw apparently logical, but actually unfounded, conclusions.

During the course of five days, the *Epidemic* manuscript was created and written down in and *around* this apartment.

That an actual epidemic was approaching during those five days, and that its awful outbreak and script completion coincided, is one of those inexplicable coincidences.

1. BACKGROUND STUDIES: Central Events Surrounding the 1918 Outbreak of the Spanish Flu in Norway

Coincident with the end of the World War I: Norway was neutral . . . or was it? Norway was pressured into a fishing trade agreement with Britain in 1916, securing Britain as the sole beneficiary of Norwegian fishing. Until then, Germany had been dependent on fish from Norway, and, enraged by this agreement, Germans retaliated with unrestricted submarine warfare in parts of the North Sea between Norway, the Faroe Islands, and Britain. In 1917, Norway lost as many as 77 ships. During World War II, 1,162 Norwegians were killed while 943 vanished at sea.

The Russian Revolution in 1917 and the establishment of the Soviet Union inspired a radicalization of Det Norske Arbeiderparti (the Norwegian Labor Party).

On 21 October 1918, Norway held parliamentary elections amid the pandemic of the Spanish Flu. It was a victory for Venstre (Liberal Party).

It was the time of the ending of monarchies and autocracies. Women's rights were on the rise with the organization of suffragettes in Britain. The first Women's Day was celebrated in Oslo in 1915, which was also the year of the first elections in which women were allowed to vote.

2. THE SPANISH FLU: *La Grippe, La Gripe Española, or La Pesadilla*

How can one understand a virus? A virus is a small infectious agent that replicates only inside the living cells of an organism. Viruses can infect all types of life forms, from animals and plants to microorganisms, including bacteria and archaea.

Fascists often use the biological metaphor: seeing *Das Volk* (the people) as a healthy body assaulted by cancers and diseases in the form of Jews, Roma, communists, and homosexuals, which need to be removed and extirpated from the healthy organism; the same goes for white supremacists ("Make America great again").

Influenza A, virus subtype H1N1—responsible for the Spanish flu, among others—is an unusually severe and deadly strain of avian influenza, known informally as "avian flu" or "bird flu" as it is caused by viruses that have adapted to birds. The Spanish flu caused an exceptional number of deaths, possibly due to the cytokine storms the disease triggered in the body, in which infected lung cells lead to the overstimulation of the immune system through the release of cytokines. This results in extensive leukocyte migration toward the lungs, causing the destruction of lung tissue and the secretion of liquid into that organ. This makes it difficult for the patient to breathe, and that could develop into pneumonia. The Spanish flu was spread by human coughing and sneezing. "The spread" is interesting as a metaphor: it could relate to war, pandemic (which also leads to quarantine), and to the spread of ideology (fascism, capitalism, or communism).

In lieu of antiviral medication, every household in Norway was prescribed alcohol as treatment against the Spanish flu. In 1918–1919, it was forbidden for shops to sell alcohol.

It is striking that the Spanish flu may have started in United States military camps and spread by warships to Europe. The first sporadic incidents of Spanish flu in Norway may have occurred in military camps at the beginning of April 1918. The first confirmed incidents occurred in Christiania (Oslo) on 15 June 1918, and were most likely transmitted from import trade ships coming from Scotland.

To avoid infection, the government and doctors encouraged proper handwashing and hygiene, and advised against congregating in huge masses of people. Schools, cinemas, assembly halls, and churches were closed for some weeks in the fall of 1918 to prevent the disease from spreading. If you got sick, you were advised to go home quickly and stay there until you got well. The flu was made a private, family matter. Many died in their beds, infecting other family members as well.

In Camus's novel, it is exactly the contrary. Once someone got sick and the doctor certified that it was plague, a protocol was activated. Police and nurses were to, first, get the sick person to the hospital and, second, quarantine the household, either by locking them up or by taking them to quarantine camps. The sick went to the hospital, most certainly to die alone, so mothers often did not report their sick children, and full households died together.

The population of Norway in 1918 was 2,565,994. Fifteen thousand Norwegian citizens died of the Spanish flu, but little over a million were infected. Tens of millions died all over the world, and some sources actually estimate as many as 50 to 100 million—3 to 5 percent of Earth's population at the time, making it the deadliest pandemic in history. Spanish flu infected an estimated 500 million worldwide, about one-third of the planet's population. And it occurred right after World War I, which had caused an estimated 9 million combatant and 7 million civilian deaths as a direct result of the war.

Survivors of the flu suffered gruesome aftereffects, writes social demographer Svenn-Erik Mamelund.[1] Norwegian society was heavily affected a long time after the pandemic was over, as most victims were between 20 and 40 years of age.

Spanish flu ripped apart many families; around five thousand households lost one or both parents, leaving many orphans behind.

Workers then struggled to get back to work. There were no longer enough workers to perform the same levels of work that had been done earlier. The ensuing chaos deepened poverty, and many were forced into the poor houses.

3. POTENTIAL CHARACTERS

The Narrator:

The narrator should be next to the action but not in it, and therefore should not be the doctor or anyone else in the story. Maybe a traveler? In *The Plague* by Camus, there is a traveler named Raymond Rambert. Rambert is a journalist visiting Oran, a town in the French colony of Algeria, to research a story on the living conditions of its Arab quarter. When the plague strikes, Rambert finds himself trapped in a city in which he feels he has no connection. But by the time an escape plan is arranged, Rambert has changed his mind. He decides to stay in the city and continue to help fight the plague. The plague, for Rambert, had the effect of a revelation: life makes sense when you make yourself responsible to your community. As we said, however, we feel the narrator should have no identity to begin with (and therefore no moral duties, no special message); this narrator would function as more of a formal strategy, a figure of storytelling, a sort of omniscient being who, at the end of the play, could become one of the characters and at that moment, have political opinions of their own. This character could be any gender, of course.

A Doctor:

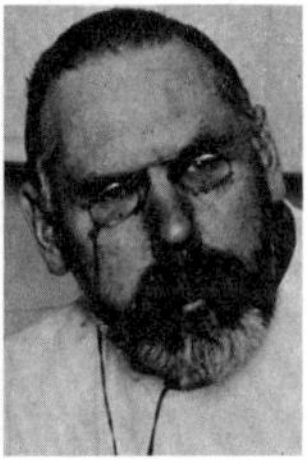

Modeled after the key protagonist of *The Plague*, Dr. Bernard Rieux. In Camus's novel, we only identify the narrator and doctor at the end of the novel. Our doctor would probably be an atheist, a practical man who works to combat the Spanish flu simply because he is a doctor, and his job is to relieve human suffering.

Probably apolitical. Reasonable. Because of this rationality, the doctor comes to ask: Why is this absurd disease mainly striking the workers and the poor? Why do some of the infected seem to be less valuable than others? Our doctor is bothered by the hypochondriac rich people of the west side of Christiania who think they are sick and take up a lot of his time.

Perhaps, in the role of the doctor: Johan Scharffenberg (1869–1965), a physician and psychiatrist practicing in Christiania from 1904 to 1919.

A Prohibitionist:
In 1916, Norway prohibited distilled beverages, and in 1917, the prohibition was extended to include fortified wine and beer. The wine and beer ban was lifted in 1923, and in 1927 the ban of distilled beverages was also lifted.

Some Politicians:
As in Camus's text, our production will feature different types of politicians. There will be those who deny the evidence of the pandemic for political reasons—there were plenty in 1918 who would not speak about the flu for fear of demoralizing the troops—and those who realize that every second counted, and that they had to act quickly, especially if a sense of solidarity pushed them to assist the poor. In the novel, this latter type takes form in the role of Jean Tarrou, a selfless adventurer, a sort of a Jack London figure convinced of the need to bring justice to suffering classes.

Some Historical Characters:

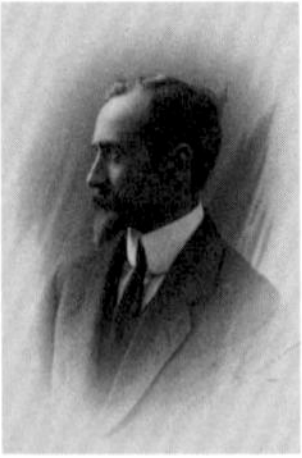

Kyrre Grepp
(1879–1922)

Chairman of the Norwegian Labor Party in 1918. It's remarkable that he died quite young, of tuberculosis at 42 years-old, only four years after he was elected.

Grepp wanted the party to join the Comintern, while his rival Martin Tranmæl did not. Grepps's death must have had an impact on the Norwegian Labor Party split that took place between 1921 and 1923. Did his sickness and poor health have any link to the Spanish flu? Was he affected? He was the rising star of the revolutionary side of the party, and yet he died prematurely.

In a 1913 speech, "Arbeiderne har intet fædreland" (The workers have no fatherland), he said: "If anyone doubts what an important force Socialism has become among Norwegians, such a doubt shall be dismissed upon seeing the strenuous efforts taken by the military to convince us Socialists to join their military endeavor."[2]

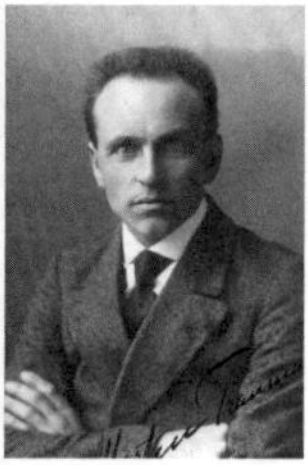

Martin Tranmæl
(1879–1967)

Public speaker and agitator, secretary for the Norwegian Labor Party. His oratory was passionate and visionary, fit to be performed in a church, and could be a powerful tool in our play.

Some of his books and pamphlets: *The Professional Means and Organizational Forms* (1911), *What the Opposition Opposes* (1913), *Who Wants Civil War?* (1915), and *Socialism and the Socialist Progress* (1918).

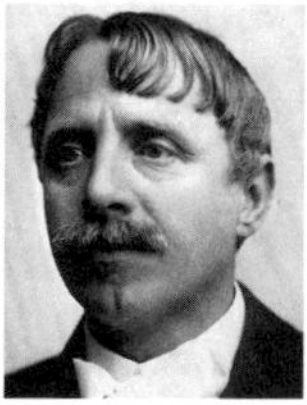

Adam Egede-Nissen
(1868–1953)

Quite the mysterious fellow. He seems to have been a favorite of Lenin, having spent the winter months of 1918 in Moscow, developing Norway's relationship to the Comintern, which would be established two months later. Marxist revolutionary Alexandra Kollontai was also a good friend—we could almost go ahead and say admirer—deeming him "Norway's first Bolshevik" in a speech that she wrote in celebration of his 70th birthday. It is said that he was among the first and most important contacts the Bolsheviks had in Norway. Egede-Nissen was also a strong supporter of prohibition in Norway.

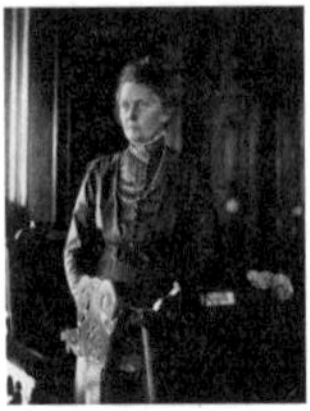

Anna Rogstad (1854–1938)

The first female member of the Norwegian Parliament, elected in 1911. In January 1917, she became a member of the Norwegian Labor Party, having come out of a more conservative and nationalistic party Frisinnede Venstre (Free-minded Liberal Party).

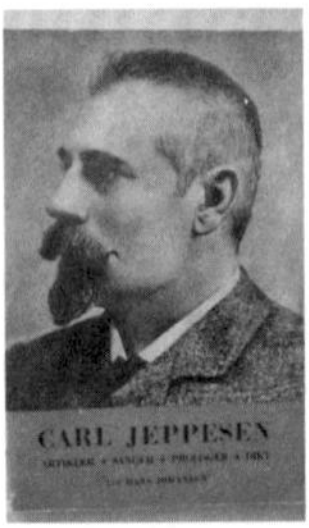

Carl Jeppesen (1858–1930)

Mayor of Christiania from 1917 to 1919. Politician, and editor of the newspaper *Social-Demokraten*. An avid smoker, he ran a cigar store. Played an essential role in building the Norwegian Labor Party. Composed songs and wrote poems.

Artists/Writers:

In Camus's text, artists are portrayed somewhat ridiculously through the character of Joseph Grand, whose only ambition is to find a good opening sentence for his new book. In *The Plague*, Grand is a 50-year-old clerk for the city government. In his spare time, he polishes his Latin and works on his book, but is such a perfectionist that he continually rewrites the first sentence and can get no further.

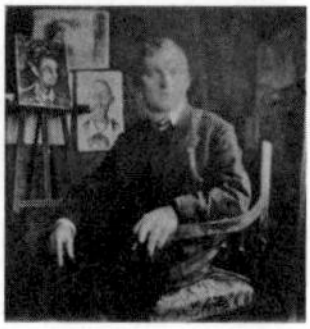

Edvard Munch
(1863–1944)

We need to turn him into a central character in the play. Really research him, use him as a visual reference as well. He is, one might say, the embodiment of Norwegianness and the country's bestselling cultural product—what Van Gogh is to the Netherlands, Munch is to Norway. He should definitely be one of our characters, but we must construct him properly: the "degenerate" artist (he was listed as an *entartete Künstler* by the Nazis), loved by the moderns, hated by the conservatives, and too hesitant to assert himself politically.

The thing about Munch is that he never actually had the plague, but he was a hypochondriac. Wondering if there is any information on how he dealt with his apparent infection, and whether or not he sought treatment? Our research brought us to this little fact about the placebo effect: it seems that the administration of false, totally ineffective drugs by doctors to patients of the Spanish flu was common. Among the most popular were aspirin (which lead to bigger problems, as taking too much aspirin fills the lungs with fluid) and alcohol. Some doctors believed that alcohol in small doses acted as a stimulant. This idea did not, perhaps, go over smoothly in the context of a prohibition movement that seemed to be gaining momentum across the Western Hemisphere, and was an explicit goal of some Norwegian Labor Party leaders, such as Tranmæl and Egede-Nissen.

Munch was 55 in 1918. Munch's contemporaries and colleagues, the Austrian expressionist painter Egon Schiele and his wife, Edith, died of the Spanish flu in October 1918. "In the autumn of 1918, the Spanish flu pandemic that claimed more than 20 million lives in Europe reached Vienna. Edith, who was six months pregnant, succumbed to the disease on 28 October. Schiele died only three days after his wife. He was 28 years old. During the three days between their deaths, Schiele drew a few sketches of Edith."[3] Maybe this can have some role in the play as well.

During the Spanish flu, Le Corbusier apparently holed up in his room and drank cognac.

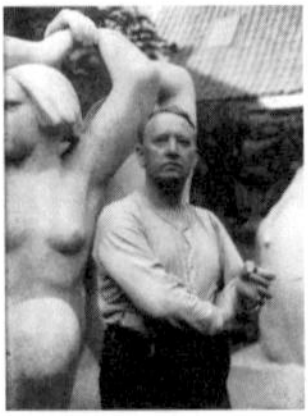

Gustav Vigeland (1869–1943)

The sculptor was 48 at the time of the Spanish flu. His rivalry with Munch related to the role of art in society. Munch would be the engaged existentialist, and Vigeland the classicist proto-fascist. In contrast with Munch, Vigeland was always praised by critics. Some art critics also considered his sculptures to be expressions of fascist aesthetics, and he has been compared to Arno Breker. Writing in *Verdens Gang*, a newspaper started by former Norwegian resistance members shortly after the German occupation of Norway, which ended in 1945, the painter and critic Pola Gauguin wrote that a Vigeland installation "reeks of Nazi mentality."[4] During the German occupation, Vigeland himself was quoted in the newspaper *Aftenposten* as stating that he was "happy" to accept prominent Nazis in his studio: "I welcome German soldiers with their excellent discipline to walk around my work."[5]

Posterity, a 2015 play by Doug Wright, imagines the interaction between Vigeland and Henrik Ibsen. This is how the character of Vigeland is described in the play: "Larpent requests that Vigeland create a bust of Ibsen. Vigeland, possessed of an ego to match Ibsen's, initially scorns the idea. But he's persuaded to undertake a commission he disdains—mere portraiture is beneath him—so he can curry favor with the culture ministry to achieve funding for his magnum opus, a sculpture depicting 'the whole of life' that will assure him the kind of immortality he craves."[6]

We can achieve a lot by playing on the antagonism between Munch, a modern, critical, conceptual, "degenerate" artist, and Vigeland, the image of academia, bourgeois ambition, and pomposity.

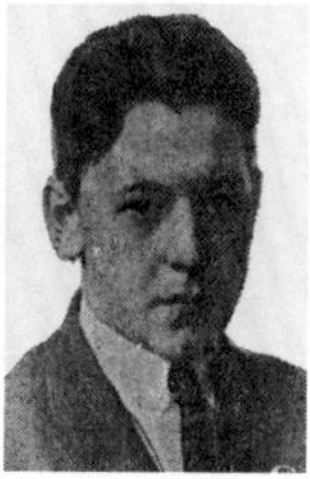

Rudolf Nilsen (1901–1929)

Writer and poet. His poems "Revolusjonens røst" (Voice of the Revolution), "Jeg hadde tenkt" (I was Thinking), and "Nr 13" (No. 13) could be worth looking at.

A child of the working class, Nilsen became part of the left-wing revolutionary movement and joined Norges Socialdemokratiske Ungdomsforbund (Social Democratic Youth League of Norway), the youth league of the Norwegian Labor Party. When the Norwegian Labor Party split in 1923 due to an ideological schism, Nilsen decided to join the youth league of the Communist Party of Norway. He died of tuberculosis in 1929.

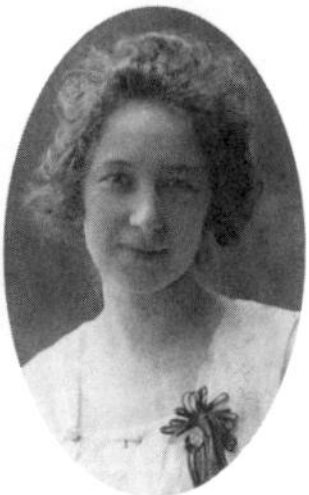

Johanne Dybwad (1867–1950)

She was the leading actress in Norwegian theater for half a century. She was also a stage director, inspired by the modernist theater movement, especially the German theater director Max Reinhardt. Worked a lot with Ibsen's contemporary plays and was an actor at Nationaltheatret in the year 1918. Would be interesting to know how the theater business reacted to the epidemic.

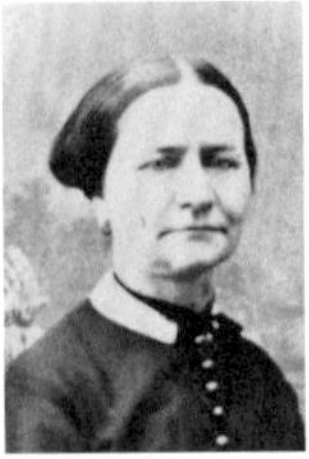

Aasta Hansteen
(1824–1908)

Aasta Hansteen was first an artist before devoting her time to the women's suffrage movement. She was a very popular portraitist but stopped because her workload made her "anxious and melancholic," it is said. To the wider world, Hansteen was a very important feminist and artist, painter, and writer. To her local contemporaries in Oslo, she was a colorful figure who walked around the city slapping (and whipping!) impertinent men, entering pubs on her own, and drinking as naturally as the next man. She died in 1908, too early for our story, but perhaps some poetic license can be taken?

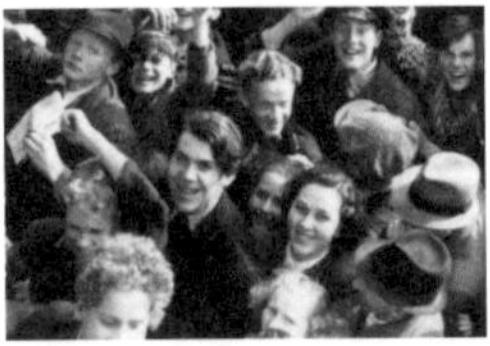

Nameless Worker:
A character in the age group that was hit hardest, those in their late twenties. A central character of the play could be a nameless worker (a convinced socialist?) with whom we can all identify, who gets the Spanish flu and dies. We can follow their struggle, trials, and tribulations throughout the play.

A Religious Fool, Prophet, or Jesus-like (or Jesuit!) Figure:
In Camus's novel, the religious zealot is Father Paneloux, a learned, well-respected Jesuit priest. He is well-known for

a series of lectures in which he championed a pure form of Christian doctrine, and chastised his audience for their laxity. During the first stage of the plague outbreak, Paneloux preaches a sermon at the cathedral. He has a powerful way of speaking, and he insists to the congregation that the plague is a scourge sent by God to those who have hardened their hearts against him. Paneloux, however, also claims that God is present to offer succor and hope. Later, Paneloux attends at the bedside of Othon's stricken son and prays that the boy may be spared. After the boy's death, Paneloux tells Rieux that although the death of an innocent child in a world ruled by a loving God cannot be rationally explained, it should nonetheless be accepted. Paneloux joins the team of volunteer workers and preaches another sermon, saying that the death of the innocent child is a test of faith. Since God willed the child's death, so should the Christian will it too. A few days later, Paneloux himself is taken ill. Trusting in God alone, he refuses to call for a doctor, and dies. Since his symptoms did not seem to resemble those of the plague, Rieux records his death as a "doubtful case."

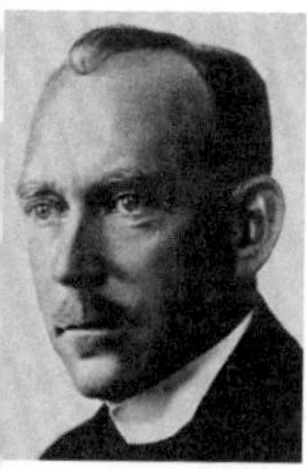

Ole Hallesby
(1879–1961)

Ole Kristian Hallesby was born in Aremark, part of the Østfold region of Norway. Hallesby grew up the sixth of eight siblings on a family farm, with a father who also served as an assistant Pietstic Lutheran pastor, of the Haugean tradition. Hallesby graduated with a degree in theology in 1903 and was awarded his doctorate in 1909. He taught at the Free Faculty of Theology from 1909 to 1952, and was chairman of the Norwegian Santal Mission from 1902 to 1906 and the chairman of Det norske lutherske Indremisjonsselskap (Norwegian Lutheran Inner Mission

Society) from 1923 to 1956. He was also central to the founding of the Norwegian Christian Student and School Association in 1924.

The prophet represents panic about the end of the world, a kind of doomsday vibe. He has seen the plague in other parts of the world, and knows of other plagues in different time periods. This prophet might be on pilgrimage to Norway? Maybe Nidaros, in Trondheim. This character has a tone of the Grim Reaper about him, and sees the plague as punishment for the revolutionary activities of the working class or the emancipation of women, perhaps sent by God. Or something else: a warning of the rise of fascism? Could be both; the Church was against German fascism (though this was not the case in Spain) since the German fascists advocated for a sort of Esoteric spirituality.

Are there any saints that can be of inspiration to this character? Bridget of Swede? Catherine of Siena? Both lived during the period of the Black Death (1347–1351).

The Choir:

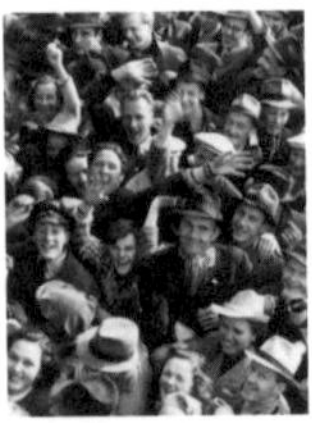

The choir is the most important character in the play. In Gerhard's opera, the choir is, undoubtedly, the people and the city. Everyone is in the choir: rich and poor, bourgeoisie and workers. The choir is Oslo, simply put. It could be the workers, a union singing workers' songs; it could be the victims of the plague.

They sing.

The Songs:

Folk songs in Norway often have a religious subject matter. They conjure piety (or fear of God) in situations marked by poverty and suffering, where death is very present in people's lives. These songs can be similar to hymns, to which they are closely related, like the one we have been rehearsing: "Dies Irae," translated as "Day or Wrath" or "Song of the Dead," is a liturgical hymn probably developed in the eleventh century.

The Helper or Good Samaritan, a Woman:

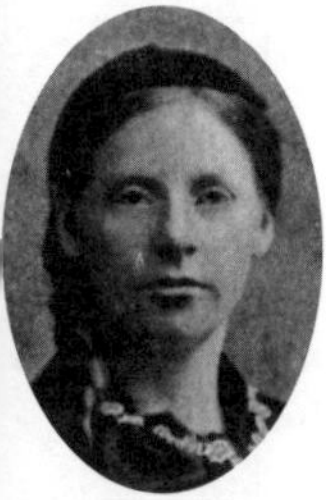

Ólafía Jóhannsdóttir (1863–1924)

A woman who devoted her life to helping the most disadvantaged in Oslo's slums at the Vaterland Bridge in the early 1900s. Has a monument erected in her honor in Oslo.

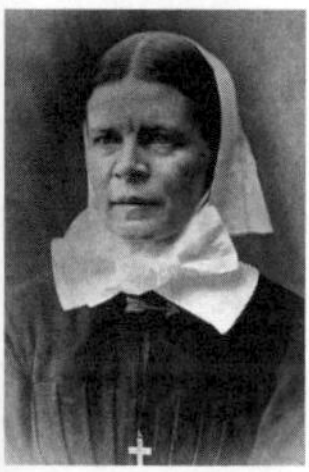

Cathinka Guldberg (1840–1919)

Norwegian nurse, educator, and deaconess. She was painted by Emmanuel Vigeland, the scorned brother of Gustav, in 1918. She educated herself as a nurse and Lutheran pastor in Germany. Returning to Norway at the age of 28, she established the Christiania Deaconess House and started Christiania's first school for nurses. She was 78 years old in 1918.

The Sick Child:

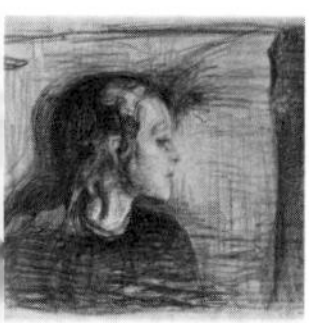

In Camus's novel, the final death, or the redeeming death, is that of the sick child, *Le petit Jacques*, the son of the magistrate. His agony is too much to bear, even for the rational doctor, and even for the faithful priest. The death of the innocent functions as a sort of Paschal Lamb (or *pharmakos*) and is the inflection point when the plague starts to recede.

Between 1885 and 1926, Munch made six paintings and a number of etchings titled *Sick Child*, depicting the agony of his sister Johanne Sophie, who died of tuberculosis at the age of 15.

4. STRUCTURE:

We have been thinking of keeping the ten-episode structure we observed in Gerhard's opera adaption of the novel by Camus; it is a good dramaturgical structure. It could be particularly powerful if combined with some visuals from or related to Munch, such as *Sick Child*.

These are the ten chapters:

I. Prologue: The City
II. First Signs (Denied)
III. First Death (Undeniable)
IV. The Name: Plague (The Politicians Admit)
V. The Doors Close—The City Isolated from the World
VI. DIES IRAE: Resistance to Death
VII. *Ubi Sunt*? The Dead Overpower the Living
VIII. The Last Death (Death of the Child) and Redemption
IX. Joy: Defeat of Death. Life Begins Again.
X. Eternal Return: The Plague Will Come Back

These could easily be adapted to explicitly refer to fascism's eternal return:

I. Prologue: The World/The Nation/Society
II. First Signs (Denied—They are not fascists, just

traditionalists)

III. First Death (Undeniable)

IV. The Name: Plague (Well, if they wear swastikas and do the Roman salute, they must be fascists after all)

V. The Doors Close—One People, One Country

VI. DIES IRAE: Resistance

VII. *Ubi Sunt*? Loss

VIII. The Last Death (Death of the Child) and Redemption

IX. Joy: Defeat of Fascism. Life Begins Again

X. Eternal Return: Fascism Will Come Back

A Potential Source for Structure and/or Choreography:

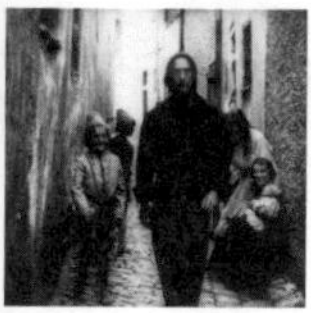

Die Pest in Florenz (The Plague in Florence, 1919), a German silent film based on Edgar Allan Poe's 1842 short story "The Masque of the Red Death." The plot takes place in Florence in 1348, at the outbreak of the Black Death. The film was directed by Otto Rippert, produced by Erich Pommer, and written by Fritz Lang. It was released in October 1919, toward the end of the Spanish flu pandemic.

1 Svenn-Erik Mamelund, *1918 pandemic morbidity: The first wave hits the poor, the second wave hits the rich*, 6 February 2018, https://www.ncbi.nlm.nih.gov/pmc/articles/PMC5907814/.

2 Jorunn Bjørgum, "Det nasjonale spørmål i norsk arbeiderbevegelse," *Tidsskrift for arbeiderbevegelsens historie*, no. 1 (1985), p. 99.

3 Wikipedia, "Egon Schiele," https://en.wikipedia.org/wiki/Egon_Schiele.

4 Pola Gauguin, "Review of the Vigeland installation," *Verdens Gang*, 3 July 1945.

5 Gustav Vigeland quoted in the newspaper *Aftenposten*, 15 April 1944.

6 Charles Isherwood, "Review: Doug Wright's 'Posterity,' a Portrait of Ibsen," *New York Times*, 15 March 2015, https://www.nytimes.com/2015/03/16/theater/review-doug-wrights-posterity-a-portrait-of-ibsen.html.

Images:

Page 159: Unknown, *Johan Scharffenberg*, photograph, courtesy Av Ukjent/Kunnskapsforlaget/NTB Scanpix; p. 160: Eivind Enger, *Kyrre Grepp*, 1921, photograph, courtesy Eivind Enger/The Norwegian Labour Movements Archives and Library; p. 161: Unknown, *Martin Tranmael*, ca. 1910, photograph, courtesy Norsk biografisk leksikon; p. 161: Unknown, *Adam Egede Nissen*, photograph, courtesy Av Ukjent/NTB Scanpix; p. 162: Anders Beer Wilse, *Anna Rogstad*, 1911, photograph, courtesy National Library of Norway; p. 162: Unknown, *Carl Jepessen*, 1935, photograph, courtesy Norsk Presseforbund; p. 163: Edvard Munch, *Self-Portrait*, 1906, photograph, courtesy Munch Museum; p. 164: Anders Beer Wilse, *Gustav Vigeland*, 1929, photograph, source: Wikipedia; p. 165: Unknown, *Rudolf Nilsen*, 1925, photograph in *Norges Kommunistblad*, source: Wikipedia; p. 165: Herman Hamnqvist, *Johanne Dybwad*, ca. 1901–1905, photograph, courtesy Oslo Museum; p. 166: H. Lunde's Fotografiske Atelier, *Aasta Hansteen*, photograph, courtesy National Library of Norway; p. 166: Unknown, Liberation Day celebration in Oslo, 8 May 1945, photograph detail, source: Radio Free Europe; p. 167: Unknown, *Ole Hallesby*, photograph, courtesy Av Ukjent/NTB Scanpix; p. 168: Unknown, Liberation Day celebration in Oslo, 8 May 1945, photograph, source: Radio Free Europe; p. 169: Unknown, *Olafía Jóhannsdóttir*, 1930, photograph, in *De ulykkelige venn* by Miriam Devold; p. 169: Postcard with a portrait of Cathinka Guldberg. ca. 1915, photo: Thea Nielsen/Nasjonalbiblioteket; p. 169: Edvard Munch, *The Sick child*, 1907, oil on canvas, Munch Museum, Oslo, courtesy Munch Museum; p. 171: Otto Rippert, *Die Pest in Florenz*, 1919, film still, source: offscreen.

Knotting Against the Machine

Natascha Sadr Haghighian

A simple drawing of a prison courtyard. High walls topped with razor wire, a watchtower pinnacling the walls in the center of the image. Two searchlights, their beams pointing downward, scan the yard in slow circular movements. Then the image starts to spin around its center, first slowly and then faster. Owing to the centrifugal forces, the drawing falls apart into lines and circles. When the rotation slows down and comes to a halt, the lines fall into place again and compose a different image. The prison courtyard has changed into a stage, framed by trusses. A single microphone stands center stage behind a prompt box. Two searchlights, their beams pointing upward, scan the stage in slow circular movements. After some moments, the image starts to spin again and the drawing yet again falls centrifugally apart into lines and circles. When the rotation slows down and finally comes to a halt, the lines have once again fallen into place, the stage is changed back into a prison courtyard. Then it spins again. And again. And again.

The incessant force of the centrifugal spin repeatedly isolates this congeries of elements, separating them into good and bad, adored and hated, chosen and excluded, artist and outcast, celebrated individual and generic criminal. While in the prison courtyard the searchlights scan the scene in anticipation of tracking and exposing an escapee, on stage the searchlights scan the scene in anticipation of tracking and exposing an artist. Two seemingly opposed concepts of exposure: while one beam of light presumes vice, the other one presumes virtue; while one beam of light exposes in order to punish, the other one exposes in order to reward. Trapped in this perpetual spin, the scenes of crime and punishment versus fame and reward become conditions of the same segregating machine.

But what are the engines that keep the centrifugal machine in constant motion? And what makes up the generators that power the searchlights and drive their tireless scanning? And, finally: What are the effects of isolating elements from a multitude? What happens to the one who gets caught in the spotlight?

The image described above is a simple drawing animated in After Effects. I made it for the Istanbul Biennial in 2001. While we were installing the show, we watched the Twin Towers in New York collapse from the Biennial offices. It was the start of the so-called War on Terror, an indefinite military campaign that has claimed necropolitical hegemony over good and bad globally without any territorial boundaries. I had intended the animation to address the dilemma that some of us were preparing for an art exhibition while others were on hunger strike in solitary confinement because of their ethnicity and political affiliation. I did not personally know anybody in Turkish prisons at the time, but from activist friends in Istanbul I knew that the architecture of solitary confinement in Turkey had been imported from the Stammheim Prison in Germany.[1] As I was invited as an artist from Germany, it seemed important to address my entanglement with those in solitary confinement. The Biennial was very wary of any link to the Kurdish struggle; I therefore had to eliminate any overt reference to it. In any case, I am not sure what I hoped the effect of my intervention would be. But what I remember clearly was the urgent need to insist on a sense of collectivity and relatedness between my "invited" body and the "banished" bodies in captivity.

After the War on Terror was launched, I developed a broader reading of the animation. With the opening of Guantanamo Bay detention camp and the use of drones for targeted killings, the haphazard isolation of "bad elements" had reached a global dimension beyond national borders. At the same time, the globalization of the art

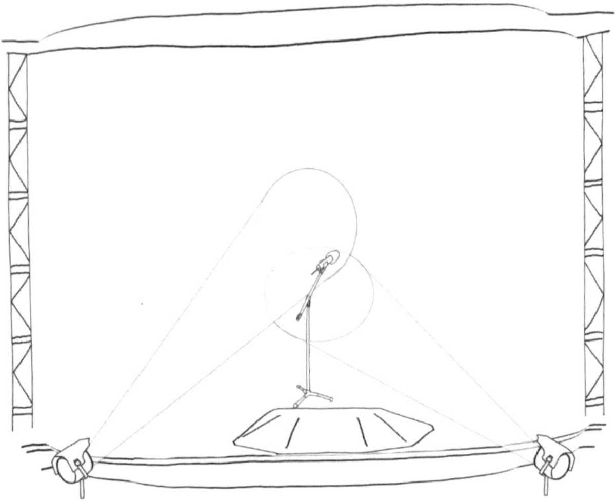

Natascha Sadr Haghighian, *Vice/ Virtue*, 2001, animation still, courtesy the artist

system allowed for ever larger stages for ever more "successful" artists. All of this feels so long ago now, but when I look at the animation now, the insidious system it depicts seems still active. An algorithmic empire is looming over our heads with its computational governance of identification, and growing detention centers and refugee camps around the word make exclusion a persistent and key feature of the current order.

I remember being taught at school what inertial forces are and what they do. My physics teacher always spluttered when he spoke and he was a groper, so I tried not to ask too many questions. But physics seemed to be important in explaining the physical world; that much I got. Something that is a law in physics, like gravity, seemed irrefutable. The forces that draft some of us as criminals and others as celebrities are treated as a form of natural

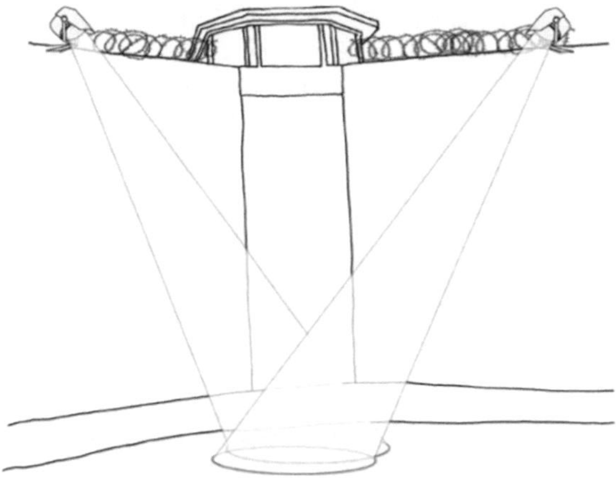

Natascha Sadr Haghighian, *Vice/Virtue*, 2001, animation still, courtesy the artist

science, as if ending up in Gitmo or at the Venice Biennale is an event of natural selection, driven by gravitational forces. And the seemingly natural response is to admire one and dread the other.

Trying to trace it back historically, this centrifugal selecting machine appears first of all as a machine of modernity. It is the machine that made the name, the individual, the nuclear family, the passport, biometrical data, visa laws, IP addresses, art prize competition, The Museum of Modern Art, Billie Eilish's bra, and the neoliberal subject that is constantly pulled away from "being with" by their affects and anxieties. This machine has been amplified through platforms like Instagram and Snapchat and has the tendency to produce totalitarian conditions in its technological dimension. Algorithmic tracking and profiling are key features of predictive policing, the fortune-telling technology of law enforcement that isolates and identifies individuals with criminal potential in an assumed future. The centrifugal machine of modernity has been straining, extracting, and deforming the collective fabric of social contracts, pulling and picking things apart, and now, in the current conditions of late liberalism, it leaves landscapes of scattered wounded individuals in broken places in its wake.

In anthropologist Elizabeth A. Povinelli's words, "the forces of straining are such and so ongoing . . . that [it] decapacitates the ability to keep oneself knotted." Keeping oneself knotted, for Povinelli, refers to collectivity as a knot, or more precisely, "it's a form of knotting in which certain spaces are able to control both the scale and circulation of the form of being in those knots."[2] To keep oneself knotted is a topological operation and hints at why certain spaces are better in maintaining forms of collectivity. In a lecture titled "After the End, Stubborn Affects and Collective Practices," Povinelli traces knotting back to Donna Haraway's situated knowledges—as an "earthwide network of connections including the ability to partially translate among very different and power differentiated communities"—and to Octavia E. Butler's writing on symbiosis and partnership. In Butler's science fiction novel *Parable of the Talents* (1998), the protagonist Lauren Oya Olamina writes in her journal: "Partnership is giving, taking, learning, teaching, offering the greatest possible benefit while doing the least possible harm. Partnership is mutualistic symbiosis. . . . Any entity, any process that cannot or should not be resisted or avoided must somehow be partnered."[3]

Looking at the animation now, I think it is crucial to understand what exactly is pulling you apart or holding you together in order to think about collaboration and develop contemporary collective (art) practices. Without an understanding of these strains, collaboration relays them to a collectivity's immanent structure and often leaves those involved disenchanted and hurt.

Povinelli has been part of the Karrabing Film Collective, a group of 25 members founded in 2008 that focuses on indigenous self-organization, social analysis, and story-telling. She never glosses over the many differences that could separate "this body"—as she designates it herself while she draws an imaginary circle above her head—from the rest of the collective. She is based in New York, and not in Australia's Northern Territory; she is Professor of Anthropology and Gender Studies at Columbia University, etc. But instead of giving in to the centrifugal forces that these differences could set into motion to draw the collective apart, she uses the privileges granted to "this body," be it access to funding, mobility, attention, and infrastructure to distribute money, invitations, and other effects of power to the collective. Difference here is not a dividing attribute; on the contrary, it adds vital elements to a collectivity if the centrifugal force is disarmed.

Philosopher and artist Bini Adamczak has laid out how capital has organized individuals into Fordist, neoliberal, or (recently again) fascist orders.[4] While under Fordism the social contract kept the regime of accumulation attractive for workers, under neoliberalism everybody was released into deregulated forms of self-management, hollowing out and dismantling the conditions for community, collectivity and trans-individual responsibilities, dependencies, and entanglements. Writer and critic Marina Vishmidt explains how the fetish of the individual, with rights to their property, their own speech, their own body, and their own creativity, was both a result of, and a compensation for, abandonment and neglect under neoliberalism. The harms of neoliberal ideology "as materialized in the conditions of everyday life," have made it easy for fascists to "organize wounded individuals who feel their individual rights are being infringed." She mentions the artist next to the citizen and the individual as the three fetishized figures whose property rights are sacrosanct.[5]

Looking at the legacy of modern art, the entire art economy is obviously a centrifugal machine around this fetish. Art's value is not countable or measurable and has been hysterically disconnected from labor. The "greatness" of a work of art is based on the idea of a unique interiority inherent in the artist. This interiority and its fetishization is the capital of the artist. Such beliefs around interiority have proven astonishingly stubborn despite the immense diversification of art practices. There have been few attempts to organize and create structures of solidarity in the arts. The common fear is still that an artist's potential would be confined or compromised by joining a collective structure.

Are the straining forces of the art economy such that they incapacitate our ability to keep ourselves knotted? How can an art practice develop not only a sense of collectivity but actual modes of collective being and making? This question obviously extends beyond art practices and even beyond the biopolitical lines of collectivity among people, extending to other life forms and other forms of existence on the planet.

I can cherish forms of retreat and solitude, but most of the time even my solitude requires some form of collectivity at some point. Otherwise there is no resonant space for practice, there is no life. Perhaps this is felt even more strongly under the global Covid-19 quarantine, in the most basic (and vital) way. As people are separated and isolated, seemingly managing their lives and practices via Zoom, they utterly depend on those bodies who harvest the crops, collect their trash, run the ICUs, care for their elders, and deliver their shopping. Is there a sense of collaboration, of collectivity, with all those bodies who cater to our survival, beyond merely clapping on our balconies? It seems obvious that the bodies that are put on the line are the ones we most depend on, yet their working conditions have been made disproportionately precarious. The contradiction shows just how rigorously basic social contracts have been dismantled and dismissed in recent decades.

Working in self-organized collaborations, coalitions, alliances, and collectives often starts with making a space. Due to the strains described above, that space is a topological one. Operating within it is a pushing and pulling, a dance within the conditions of the status quo in which pockets of joyful survival can appear in the forms of experience, encounter, and spending time. That is where the knotting starts and where unsegregated space is maintained. The challenge, then, is to avoid making that space another interiority and drawing borders around it. While trust, generosity, and intimacy are crucial, the strains are such that the group dynamic can lead to exclusivity and enclosure. Temptations come at many levels; a "successful" collaboration can be fetishized as easily as an individual or a brand.

How to knot—how to think and form collectivity and self-organization—is key to my practice and I have collected experiences through many different collective efforts. In my experience the different forms of collectivity each have distinct dynamics and pitfalls. Hence clarity in the choice of form and structure helps strengthen the knot, and most of the time, the health of those involved.

The goals of organizing also benefit from this clarity, I have found. I want to share some examples here of coalitions and alliances consisting of different groups and individuals from the arts and from activism. They are specific in that they all have clear aims. This is important to mention, as I consider knotting with less "obvious" aims equally important but perhaps harder to recount. Knotting for pleasure and joy, knotting for studying together, and knotting for survival can all take many forms.

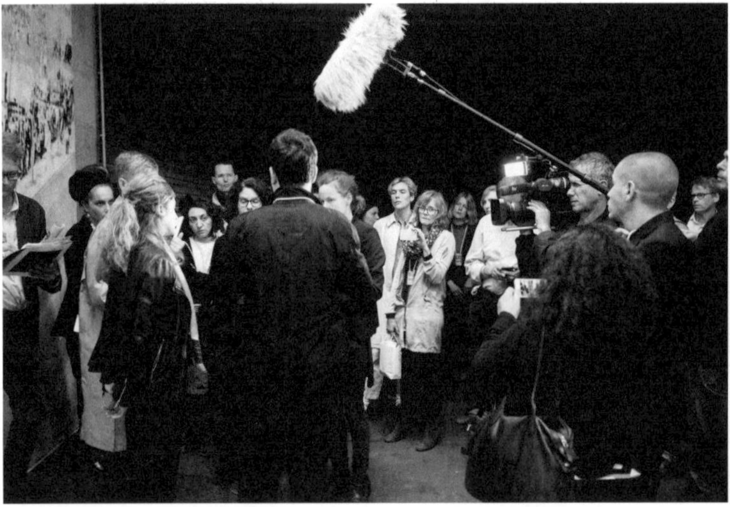

The Society of Friends of Halit, press conference, Neue Neue Galerie (Hauptpost), documenta 14, 2017, photo: Fred Dott

The Gulf Labor Coalition

The Gulf Labor Coalition is a self-organized group of artists, writers, architects, curators, and other cultural workers who are trying to ensure that workers' rights are respected during the construction of new cultural institutions on Saadiyat Island (the "Island of Happiness"), in Abu Dhabi. Gulf Labor has been active since 2011 to highlight the coercive methods of recruitment and the deplorable living and working conditions of migrant laborers who are building the Guggenheim Abu Dhabi, the Louvre Abu Dhabi, and the Sheikh Zayed National Museum (in collaboration with the British Museum) on Saadiyat Island. The coalition demands contractual guarantees that will protect the rights of workers employed in the construction and maintenance of the newly-built museums.

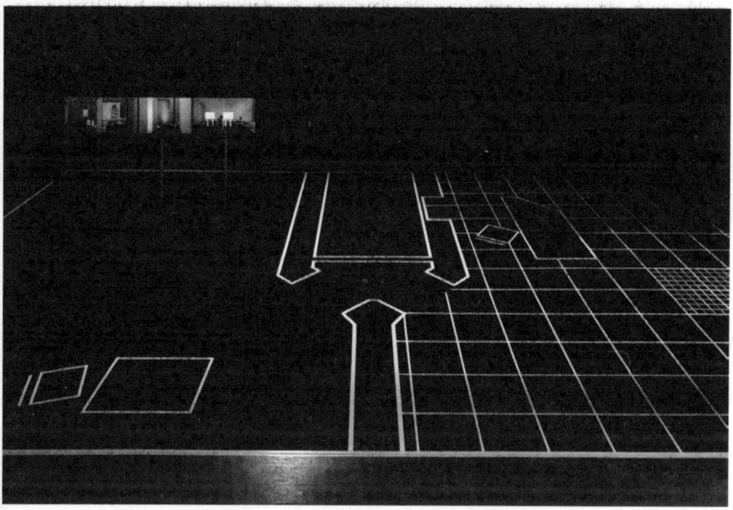

Forensic Architecture, *77sqm_9:26 min*, 2017, installation view, BAK, basis voor actuele kunst, Utrecht, photo: Tom Janssen

Tribunal "Unraveling the NSU Complex"

The Tribunal "Unraveling the NSU Complex" is a people's tribunal initiated and organized by a large coalition of anti-racist and migrant rights networks, groups, and individuals in Germany and globally in response to revelations about the so-called

National Socialist Underground (Nationalsozialistischer Untergrund, NSU), a German neo-Nazi terrorist organization. The tribunal calls upon "an open society of the many, cultivated through migration,"[6] and demands the unraveling of structural and institutional racisms. It joins the families and friends of the victims of NSU terror in their accusation of organs of the state and their institutional complicity in the NSU Complex, and speaks out against the silencing of those who have been targeted and affected by it. The term "NSU Complex" is used to describe the composite of neo-Nazi terror and institutional and structural racism. The tribunal is a continuous process with the first having taken place as the People's Tribunal "Unraveling the NSU Complex" over the course of four days in Cologne in May 2017. During this inaugural tribunal, a number of hearings, testimonies, and presentations were held, along with various workshops, group meetings, exhibits, and discussions.

The Society of Friends of Halit

The Society of the Friends of Halit is an alliance that was founded to re-narrate histories and target institutional and structural racism through self-organized investigations. It formed within the working context of the People's Tribunal "Unraveling the NSU Complex" as part documenta 14's public program, Parliament of Bodies. The Society consists of various groups, initiatives, and individuals whose work is devoted to anti-racist and anti-fascist research and organizing. During documenta 14 it presented an exhibition at the former *Hauptpost* (main post office), with contributions by Forensic Architecture, Initiative 6. April, the People's Tribunal "Unraveling the NSU Complex," and spot_the_silence that specifically addressed the killing of Halit Yozgat in Kassel and the presence of secret service agent Andreas Temme during the murder.

1 See Peter Nowak, Gülten Sesen, Martin Beckmann, eds., *Bei lebendigem Leib. Von Stammheim zu den F-Typ-Zellen. Gefängnissystem und Gefangenenwiderstand in der Türkei* (Münster: Unrast Verlag, 2001).

2 Elizabeth A. Povinelli, "After the End, Stubborn Affects and Collective Practices" (lecture, Sonic Acts Festival, Amsterdam, 24 February 2019), https://vimeo.com/322749834.

3 Octavia E. Butler, *Parable of the Talents* (1998; repr., New York: Grand Central Publishing, 2007), p. 135.

4 Bini Adamczak, "Die Versprechen der Gegenwart (The Promises of the Contemporary)" (lecture, *Propositions #9: Deserting from the Culture Wars*, BAK, basis voor actuele kunst, Utrecht, 15 November 2019), https://www.youtube.com/watch?v=TRZAGmJZG38.

5 Marina Vishmidt, lecture as part of the panel "Counter-histories," White West: The Resurgence of Fascism as a Cultural Force, ~~La Colonie~~, Paris, 9 May 2018.

6 See *Tribunal NSU-Komplex auflösen* (Tribunal "Unraveling the NSU-Complex"), https://www.nsu-tribunal.de/en/.

Remembering the Future

Kader Attia

> In modern countries . . . in Europe or elsewhere in the world . . . the streets are named after dead people. We travel through the arteries of the dead. The world in which we live is a kind of psychological tomb where dead people live on as ghosts.[1]

This observation by the Tunisian psychoanalyst Fethi Benslama, which he makes in my film *Reflecting Memory* (2016), suggests a permanent proximity to the world of the dead that requires us to listen to their calls. Of what traces are the dead the name? What are these traces asking? Why are these phantoms not at peace? Our contemporary world is haunted by wounds from the past. The traumas resulting from the worst moments in history (wars, famines, genocides) have left lasting material and incorporeal scars, which, like the phantom limb of an amputated body part, are still there. They demand reparation.

"Remembering the future" sounds paradoxical because remembrance refers to a time that has already happened. But what if our future were nothing but a continuum of injuries, the reading of which depends on our ability to maintain a thread of ethics between what we have experienced individually and collectively, and what we need to address to repair them? This would be a schizophrenic future in which the events of the past and those of the present seem to be all too familiar from our memory.

Legacies and Genealogies

To try and draw the genesis of contemporary fascism, let's go back to the 1990s—that strangely premonitory decade, stuck in between the neoliberal cynicism of the 1980s and 9/11, which introduced us to a bloody twenty-first century that had barely begun. The 1990s is a decade that rarely comes to our mind when we try to understand the return of yesterday's demons. The occurence of 9/11 has

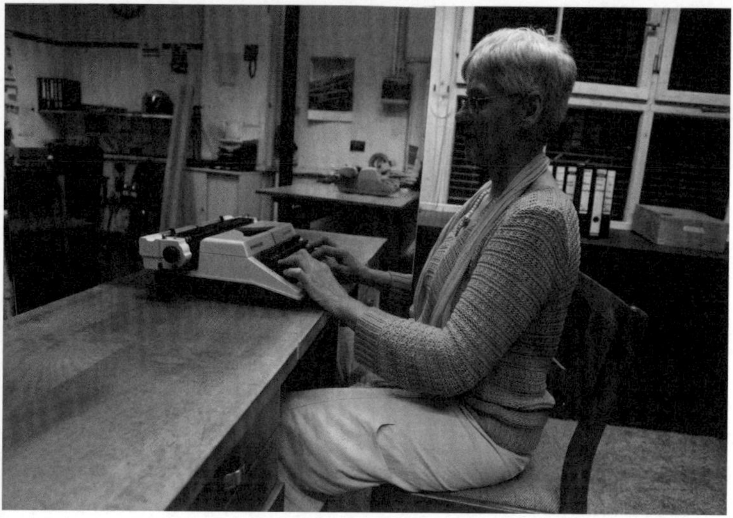

Kader Attia, *Reflecting Memory*, 2016, video still, courtesy the artist, Galleria Continua, Galerie Krinzinger, Lehmann Maupin, and Galerie Nagel Draxler

often been regarded as a symptom of the accelerated extraction of value from the West's former colonies blowing up in the face of neoliberalism. However, this diagnosis fails to address how radical Islam abets capitalism even while attacking its symbolic core. Such complicity should come as no surprise: because capitalism has no ideology, it adapts itself to anything that sustains its growth, even conflicting ideologies; all of the most widely practiced religions today have embraced capitalism. Such porosity is also open to arrangements with fascism in periods of socioeconomic disorder in the old imperial centers. After World War I, when Walter Benjamin was reflecting on capitalism and religion, Europe was to fall under the sway of this ideology that promised restoration of privileges—based on "scientific" demonstrations of racial superiority—to rattled and embattled whites.

How have European fascisms, which we believed were destroyed forever, been reborn from their ashes? How have we allowed ourselves to be surprised again? Here we need to go back in time just a little bit further than the 1990s. European political modernity was born from the ancient Greek model of democracy. This model has of course been totally idealized by Enlightenment thought, which viewed it as a "paradise for all" when Athens was in fact a slave society—and where, even among non-slaves, only adult male citizens could vote. Invoking the legacy of ancient Greek democracy for the European political project requires coming to terms with this dirty little truth. Incidentally: when the French Revolution tried to get serious about the Enlightenment idea of human rights, abolishing slavery in France and its colonies in 1794 (after the slaves of Saint-Domingue had already started their own revolution), Napoleon Bonaparte attempted to bring it back in 1802.

The genesis of European political modernity is not only defined by Athens' political structures or political thought (such as Plato) but also by its popular culture—by the theater, not only the agora. Aristotle wondered why Greeks would gather in their tens of thousands in ancient theaters. He came to the conclusion that they went to the theater to experience the pleasurable pain of catharsis; experiencing terror and fear, the citizens could purge their emotions and allow themselves to heal.

Tragedy as a healing ritual is fundamental to understanding the power of the wide range of emotions provided by catharsis as conveyed by charismatic political figures. When they perform, charismatic actors or politicians can rally millions of people around them, merged into a mass that belongs to them. If this experience of a crowd hypnotized by a belligerent voice is linked to the democratic model, which Europe has been fighting for since the beginning of the nineteenth century, then it is easy to understand the limits of this system that the worst tyrants have exploited to their advantage. Politics in the age of mass media—and now of social media—is *the agora as theater.*

Back to the 1990s. While the left had largely abandoned the field of emotion since the 1970s, one Italian politician stepped into the breach, becoming prime minister for the first time (with a short-lived cabinet) in 1994, and dominating this and the following decade. Silvio Berlusconi slowly conquered the Italian people by galvanizing them through the populist media that he himself had created in the early 1980s. He became a political force because he understood that the capitalist tool that had made him rich would also allow him to grab political power: the media, particularly television. Through populist speeches, fake news, and controversial slogans, he brought himself to the attention of the majority of the lower and middle classes, who identified with his rhetoric reeking of fascism.

The abandonment of the field of emotion, in Italy and elsewhere in Europe, also meant neglecting the role of catharsis in politics and culture. In France, the left cut itself loose from the people shortly after coming to power in 1981. It became economically social democratic (which is to say: technocratic) and culturally snobbish. In French, we call the proponents of such developments "*la gauche caviar*" or "champagne socialists." During the 1980s, both so-called elite and popular culture came to neglect the truth of the form, the noise, the smell, the texture—anything that would scream pain and warning about our world drifting away. These years witnessed the increasing market and media success of contemporary art: a (post-) conceptual art cut off from reality, avoiding deep emotions

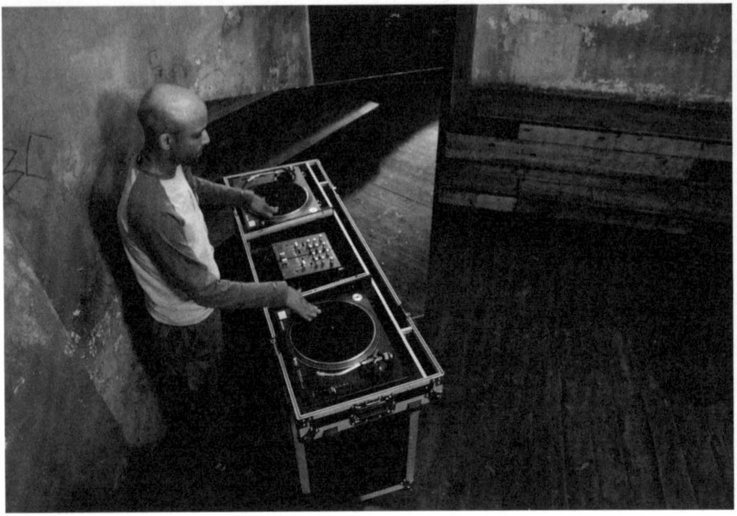

Kader Attia, *Reflecting Memory*, 2016, video still, courtesy the artist, Galleria Continua, Galerie Krinzinger, Lehmann Maupin, and Galerie Nagel Draxler

and tailor-made for speculation. Since art is a non-regulated market, fortunes made during yuppie years, thanks to the neoliberal economy and the widening social divide, were invested in a non-emotional art that turned a blind eye to the suffering of the world—a political reality born from the neoliberal disaster.

Reappropriating the Field of Emotion

Since the 1990s, as before in the 1920s and 1930s, the conquest of the field of emotion has become the main stake in Europe and in much of the Western world (and beyond). If there is a way we can stand against fascism today, it is by reappropriating the field of emotion—through activism, culture, and psychology. Theory is, of course, needed to map contexts and elaborate strategies, but it is not enough. Art and action are the ways we can reappropriate the field of emotion to heal the immaterial injuries that our European

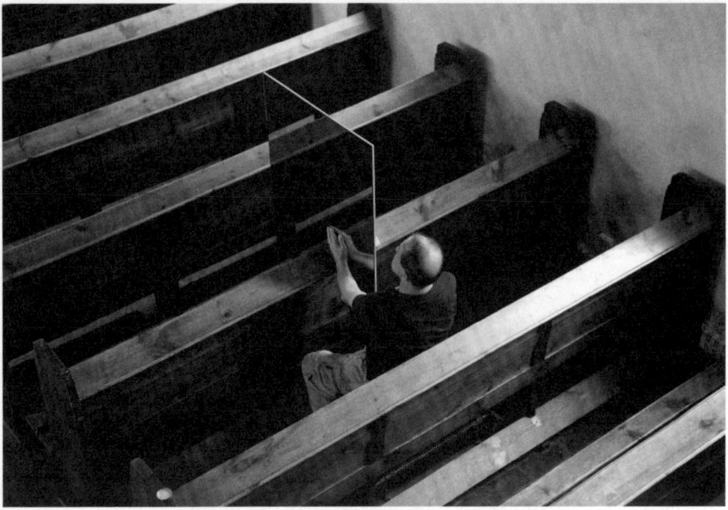

Kader Attia, *Reflecting Memory*, 2016, video still, courtesy the artist, Galleria Continua, Galerie Krinzinger, Lehmann Maupin, and Galerie Nagel Draxler

society has never managed to repair. The dark legacy of these injustices—discrimination against racialized people of all kinds, discrimination based on gender, religion, and so on—have barely been acknowledged in the national narratives and still aren't in the public psyche. European racism has always forced the others, from Jews to Arabs to Muslims, into the position of subalterns. Today, Islamophobia and anti-Semitism are once again freely expressed at varying levels of public visibility and institutional prestige.

So, how can we reappropriate the field of emotion? If the term "reappropriation" raises questions and evokes an anarchist as well as a Marxist focus on property and on expropriating the capitalists, my focus is on reclaiming the sphere of affect, desire, and fear—which has indeed increasingly been privatized and made productive. We have always been controlled through intimate weakness, from ancient Greek theater to Goebbels' speeches, but now our correlative addiction to the narrative of our fears and hopes has mutated into a massive scale of emotional reproduction that aims at anticipating our intimate behaviors. Through the likes of Cambridge Analytica, humans worldwide are losing the power of being unpredictable.

Under such conditions, reappropriating the field of emotion means creating social links in an increasingly digitized world. Modern urbanism and population management have long fostered the disappearance of human physicality in social relations, prioritizing technology instead. Using public transportation, you behave automatically every day, almost without paying attention to your environment. This mechanization of our lives is today accelerating into an artificial intelligence agency that controls the human flux in cities. AI is realizing the dreams of those architects and politicians who were obsessed with control and prediction, enhancing the colonization of our everyday life. What Michel Foucault—who by over-attacking the institution, created the bed for neoliberalism—has criticized as biopolitics are now back through the technoliberal regime of recycling public to private institutions that also control us (Apple, Amazon, Google, Facebook, etc.). Nowadays, artificial intelligences are colonizing our everyday life and psyche, exactly as biopolitics do. If we want to seize control of our lives and our connections to others, we need to reappropriate our power of interpretation—the interpretation of yesterday, today, and tomorrow. The future of Europe's past also lies in the ability to rethink what was relevant yesterday and what is not anymore. That's why I have dreamed of a space where we could experiment with counterreactions to the current disappearance of human connection and the uniformization of diversity, and to free both memory and speech.

The result is ~~La Colonie~~, located in Paris in front of the Gare du Nord train station, in a neighborhood where you don't need to investigate the history of the location to understand that colonialism still weighs heavily on French society. Because I have grown up in a post-colonial environment, belonging to a community that was invisible within the academic arena, I became very sensitive to the silence, the absence, the denial imposed on us. I have always dreamed of a space that would be *our* space, and where *we* could deconstruct the repressive narrative system in which we are the objects. ~~La Colonie~~ is an agora of intimate counter-theater that aims at repairing the absence, the lack of acknowledgment, and the very loud silence that still kills today. Because, of course, silence kills. Silence has always killed.

How does ~~La Colonie~~ try to elaborate strategies of fugitivity and futurity in our society of control, surveillance, and denial? Affect articulates the orientation of a society, socially and psychologically, between the individual and the collective along trajectories that go back and forth through art, media, and politics. The field of emotion can be reappropriated by the forging of social connections, through activism and culture, and by questioning the genealogies of contemporary issues. At ~~La Colonie~~, as well as in my documentaries, I have engaged different psychologists, psychoanalysts, and psychiatrists in political and historical conversations. Algerian psychiatrist Karima Lazali is one of them. Her essay about "the colonial trauma" is one of the most accurate investigations of the painful legacy of colonialism today.[2] While Lazali works as a psychoanalyst with racialized people in Paris and with Algerians in Algeria, she has diagnosed the traumas of contemporary Algerian society not from her clinical experiences but rather from literature and printed media.

Texts by writers such as Kateb Yacine or Mohammed Dib and articles and anonymous letters published in Algerian newspapers both during and after the colonial period have helped her to understand the political strategies of colonialism: specifically the slips, neologisms, missing words, and overdetermined sentences in these writings.[3] For example, in one sentence from Albert Camus's unfinished novel *Le premier homme* (The First Man), a colonizer says, a few days before independence, "If what we did here is a crime, then we must erase it."[4] This erasure announces and legitimizes the continuation of the colonial project and its hegemony over the psyche and the culture of the occupied, underlying the impunity still granted to the colonizers. While populating their cities with their own dead, the colonizers erase everything in the colonies, from family names to cities. Even craft brotherhoods were forbidden by law, under the ruse that they were fronts for resistance against the invaders.

Psychoanalysts such as Lazali and Fethi Benslama, who form the Arabophone Psychoanalysts' Society, have been invited to share their work and discuss it with the public at ~~La Colonie~~. As often happens in France when people talk publicly about colonialism, these debates were polarized between decolonial thought and the denial of colonialism as a crime, but at least there was a debate and social links were forged or modified. The reappropriation of the field of emotion needs such symbolic actions to make visible the repressed injuries that call for repair.

~~La Colonie~~ opened on 17 October 2016: a significant date in the history of the fight against colonialism. On that day in 1961, Algerian migrants in France demonstrated for the freedom of their homeland. My father was a participant. The demonstration, a peaceful march along the Seine, was repressed by the police with extreme violence. The men and women at the front of the march were thrown into the river,

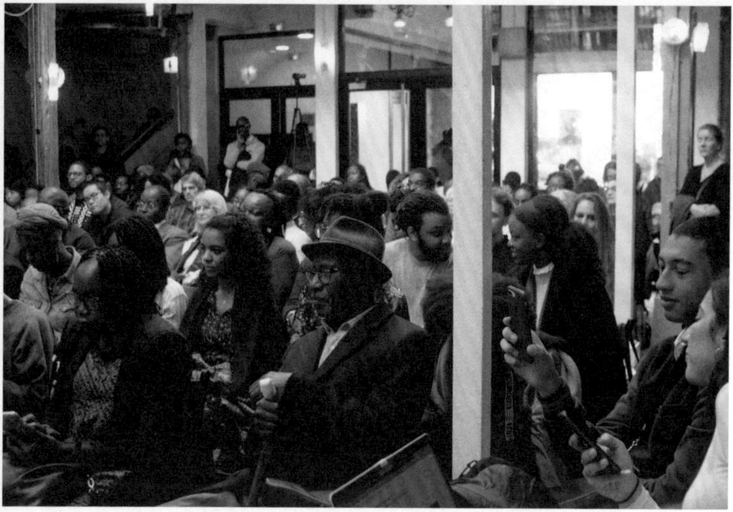

An event at La Colonie, Paris, 2019, photo: Alix Hugonnier

handcuffed. More than 262 protesters drowned. Until now, this police massacre has never been officially acknowledged as a crime committed by the French state; on the contrary, perpetual denial has been the state's response to so many claims by the survivors and their descendants. Each 17 October we organize a debate at La Colonie to rewrite and reappropriate the narrative of this sinister colonial event. By doing so, we try to maintain the memory of the people who died and their fight through public dialogues with French and Algerian activists who took part in the demonstration—like the artist Jean-Jacques Lebel—who was among the French artists and intellectuals who publically supported Algerian independence and denounced the use of torture by the French Army.[5]

In these meetings, we also share the microphone with the public, including survivors who have spent almost 60 years in silence. I remember a man of small stature whose coat was bigger than he was, but who had an incredible intensity when he said: "I was there, and as you can see, I don't have a big body, so I could escape the cops when they tried to put me in handcuffs. I saw an endless flow of bodies thrown into the Seine river. I saw them dying. As you maybe don't know, many of the Algerian migrants came from the countryside of Algeria and had never learned to swim." Right after him, another man took the microphone and began with a self-deprecating joke:

> Even if I look old, I am younger than him, young enough to not have been part of this demonstration. I was five years old when it happened. But what I remember is what we heard and saw with my father a week after when, at the 19th arrondissement police station, in front of 21 big black plastic bags, we had to identify the body of my sister Nadia Beddar, the youngest Algerian freedom activist who was part of the demonstration. She was 17, and since then our family has had to live with the official reason of her death that was given to us, which was that she had been killed by her "pimp." Until today I have lived with this burden, and I am so grateful to be able to speak here and share my experience of this crime committed and denied by the state.

As the psychoanalyst Gražina Gudaitė states in an interview for my film *Reflecting Memory*, "The complex of inferiority is never too far from the individuals who have been suffering from a collective political trauma. Fascist discourses use that weakness to reactivate fear, anger, emotion." In a different way, the postcolonial body embodies this same pain. Each individual's psyche and body has been weakened in order to be controlled. This strategy of vulnerabilization also takes the form of state crimes, such as everday violence and killings by police against descendants of the colonized.

One debate at ~~La Colonie~~ presented the audience with the case of Théo Luhaka, one of the most significant cases of harassment on the body of a postcolonial citizen—a continuation of the treatment meted out to his ancestors. On 2 February 2017 at 4:53 pm, Luhaka—a French man of Congolese origin, then 22 years old—was going home after soccer training when five French police officers, who had been controlling another group of young people, started to insult and attack him. When they suddenly tried to pull him to the ground, he resisted. Four policemen jumped on him and beat him, and the fifth fired pepper-spray less than 50 cm from his face, despite the can's strict warning against spraying less than 2 meters from the eyes. The police carried on with the aggression until one of them violently inserted his truncheon into the anus of Luhaka, who collapsed immediately. Though his body was barely moving, the police continued to beat and insult him. Brought to the hospital, Luhaka needed emergency surgery as his anus had been ripped apart.

If the physical crime is clear here, the moral one has been endlessly disputed on TV, in newspapers, and on social media, by politicians from the far right to the far left, none of them caring about Luhaka's dignity, all refusing to accept his claim that he was violently raped. The French judiciary has even asked Luhaka to prove his innocence, instead of asking the police to prove theirs, even after the release of three CCTV videos clearly showing five heavily weaponized police beating a single man and raping him. Fifteen days after the event, ~~La Colonie~~ was the only space in France to welcome Luhaka's parents and his close friends, as Théo himself was

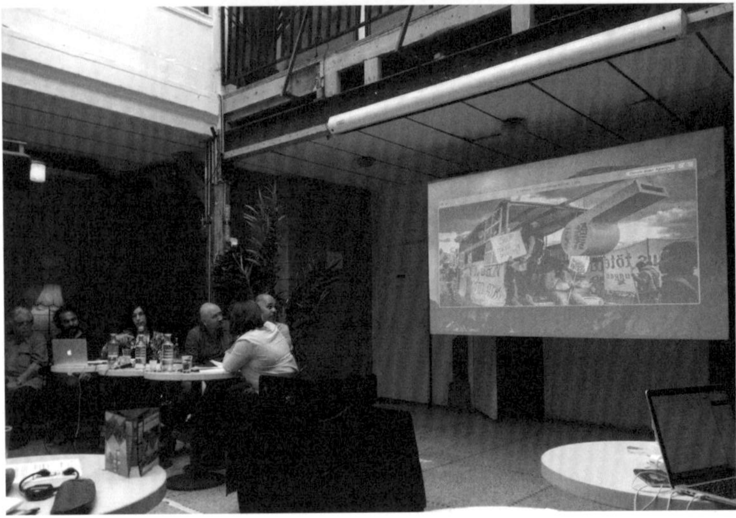

Panel "Necropolitics" during symposium White West: The Resurgence of Fascism as a Cultural Force, ~~La Colonie~~, Paris, 9 May 2019, photo: Sven Lütticken

still in the hospital. In the wake of this event, some of his friends were part of a group that decided to create their own media: an online TV channel named Paroles d'Honneur ("words of dignity" or "honor") in reaction to the monopoly of the official narrative on this affair, which has always made Luhaka the guilty party, the aggressor when police officers were only doing their job.

The reappropriation of the media and of dominant narratives is one important way of reclaiming the field of emotion, and that's why ~~La Colonie~~ has supported this group of young people, offering them a space to record some of their programs. In addition to this, I decided to make a film, *The Body's Legacies: The Post-Colonial Body* (2018), about what is shown in these CCTV videos and to collaborate with Luhaka's friends and activists from Paroles d'Honneur. The French state and media continue the colonial project by invisibilizing descendants of the colonized as long as they refuse to merge into the uniformizing narrative of the French state, called "assimilation." The reassertion of the dignity of being different while at the same time being French or European is crucial to the construction of a common ground, an "us," to which projects like ~~La Colonie~~ concretely contribute.

Because the racism we are witnessing today from East to West—especially here in Europe—has deep roots in our history, we need to remember our own irreparable mistakes. The inequality and poverty generated by neoliberalism, which intensify fears of the future, fuel the activities of ultranationalist groups that are bringing back powerful institutional fascism in Europe. In a world in which the neoliberal economy has triumphed and in which so-called representative democracy does not represent the people, who instead run to social media to be informed and entertained, we need to support collective action in shared physical space and to create avenues by which we can reappropriate the field of emotion.

"Remembering the future" suggests an endless particular loop reflecting the future as an inception, the beginning of a consciousness formed by the need for reparation. When I chose this title, I was thinking about a possible tangible future that takes care of injuries that have never been healed. "To remember" means to record, but the combination of the prefix "re-" with "membering" also suggests the return of the "member" that was missing. Like a phantom limb that calls endlessly for a return to its original location, remembering the future means loyalty to the event that has been amputated from the ostracizing narrative of the rulers.

1 Kader Attia, *Reflecting Memory*, 2016, video, 40 min.

2 Karima Lazali, *Le trauma colonial: Une enquête sur les effets psychiques et politiques contemporains de l'oppression coloniale en Algérie* (Paris: La Découverte, 2018), p. 88.

3 Ibid.

4 Albert Camus, *Le premier homme* (1960; repr., Paris: Gallimard, 1994), p. 168. Translation by author.

5 See, for instance, Jean-Jacques Lebel's involvement in a collective painting against French colonial warfare in Algeria, *Le Grand Tableau antifasciste collectif* (1960), http://www.algeriades.com/le-grand-tableau-antifasciste/article/le-grand-tableau-antifasciste.

The Invisible Culture Wars

Geert Lovink (in conversation with Sven Lütticken and Esmee Schoutens)

Sven Lütticken: In the context of this publication, I believe it would be worthwhile to reflect on your involvement in critical media studies and initiatives from the 1980s until today. In the 1980s and early 1990s, you were part of the theory collective Bilwet, also known as Adilkno, which theorized (historical and ongoing) fascisms as well as the media, though it is mostly known as a media theory outfit.[1] The heyday of Bilwet's activity also saw the Reagan/Bush-era culture wars, with the right-wing rhetoric about political correctness; from here, one can draw a line to today's attacks on "woke" culture, feminism, and "gender ideology," etc. The tactical media scene of the 1990s has also seen some maneuvers appropriated in the insurgent politics of today's alt-right. Through some genealogical digging I hope we can tease out the interrelation of several of these moments.

I was struck by a passage in the manifesto "The ABC of Tactical Media," which you co-authored with David Garcia in 1997, that reads as follows: "The revolution in consumer electronics and expanded forms of distribution (from public access cable to the internet) are exploited by groups and individuals who feel aggrieved by or excluded from the wider culture."[2] I was wondering if you could comment on this from a contemporary point of view, since I believe this resonates today with those who feel aggrieved by or excluded from the wider culture from a far-right, fascist position. And secondly, restating a question that was brought up in 2017 at The Society of Post-Control symposium, whether you see any "new opportunities for progressive emancipatory politics that are able to surf the chaos as effectively as the insurgent populists of the new right (alt-right and beyond)?"[3]

Geert Lovink: To me this goes back to a chicken-and-egg question of what comes first: media awareness and counter-concepts, which then lead to social movements, or a counterculture, which then leads to an infrastructure to spread information and further awareness? This is the question of the origin of the counter-discourse as a lively and lived one: it is the way people talk, dress, and behave, but it is also embedded in counter-information. Coming from the 1960s, my fellow media activists and I concluded that an attack on the hegemonic forces needed to be solid and fueled by research and self-organization. In other words, counter-information cannot just be put out there but has to be developed by collectives, groups, and movements. This is a labor point of view that is embedded in spaces and connected places, such as printing houses, magazines, pirate radio stations, film and video collectives, magazines and pamphlets, alternative archives, spaces where groups can meet freely, cafés, bike repair places, bookshops, cinemas, theaters, concert halls, and exhibition spaces. One can organize such spaces as one-off pop-up events, but this is not the idea of a social movement. We claim and occupy space and time, which are interrelated if you want to enforce and implement radical change.

Within this landscape, tactical media is only a tiny subcategory, for instance, of the appropriation of consumer media. It is important to note that this is not about the behavior of individuals; it is about bringing things to a higher organizational level to further collective knowledge. Within this scene we did not want to reproduce certain formats and discourses but wanted to break through conventions and question everything.

From Fascism to Media

SL: There is a beautiful segment in your essay "Requiem for the Network," written for the 2020 catalog of the Berlin transmediale festival, in which you note that "platforms establish a psychic blockade to think and act. . . . Their 'service design' is such that we're no longer lured into taking action. Instead, we express our outrage or concern. These are the 'networks without a cause' that invite us to respond to each and every event with a stripped-down opinion, basic signs, responses."[4] This focus on subjectivity and subjectivation can already be found in some of the early Bilwet texts, for instance in "Victorious, Lost, Permanent War," co-written with Bas-Jan van Stam in 1984.[5] You wrote: "The personal is no longer the place where the counterforce manifests itself, but the place where power is shaped. . . . The new war is all about an inner front where the battle is played out of the liberation and mobilization of desires and feelings."[6] This inner front is the last front, the final frontier—and here we are.

> **GL:** At the time it was perhaps rather abstract because there was no "real" war taking place in Western Europe, although information warfare was definitely happening, which Paul Virilio called "pure war." The year 1984 is also the year that marks the birth of the "user," or the subject as (computer) user. It is not only the year of George Orwell but also the year of the launch of the Apple Macintosh—remember how Steve Jobs brought these two together in that spectacular Orwellian television ad?

SL: The 2019 *Bilwet Fascismemap* (Adilkno Fascism Folder) consists of a collection of essays from 1983 to 1994, unpublished at the time, with a focus on the conjunction of fascism and sexism; sexism rooted in patriarchy and heteronormativity.[7] Your reflections issue from a culture of male feminist groups, of which the reactionary men's rights group of the Jordan B. Peterson and Thierry Baudet era seem like a dystopian mockery.

GL: This anthology goes back to the West German psychohistorian Klaus Theweleit. His publication *Male Fantasies* (1977–1978) was the prime text for Bilwet's political and theoretical work.[8] But, of course, also Michel Foucault's notion of "non-fascist life," which is directly connected to Theweleit's work. Struggles must always have a blueprint of a lived alternative (not merely a utopia) in them, otherwise they simply mirror the status quo in their resistance. Anti-fascism is not enough; we must uphold and beat the fascists, but this militancy must be backed-up by active forms of deconstruction of the authoritarian character, hate speech, and discrimination. The idea here was to eliminate the root causes of fascism rather than just fight some symptoms out on the streets. From the very beginning, the "male liberation movement" had two faces. It was a response to the strong autonomous forms of self-organization of the feminist movement and, on the other hand, also an effort to give a positive spin to male self-organization. But the male movement was acutely aware of the ambivalent form of the male-only organization, as this is the core of patriarchy—Bilwet was one such male-only group. Unfortunately, the history of this male liberation movement of the late 1970s and early 1980s has not yet been written. I personally did not play a role in this movement, apart from our intense reception of Theweleit that we used as model. The question here is still relevant today: Who is going to dismantle power, and how? How do you take it apart and not just replicate it once you take over? Removing people from their positions is often merely symbolic. Changing the laws is considered a joke in this respect, as behavioral patterns, written into actual bodies, will not be "regulated" by lawyers and other police forces. The invocation of "rights" is a passive-aggressive gesture. If power is deeply embedded in culture—the dominant late twentieth century assumption—then we will have to come up with fundamentally different ideas of what politics can do.

By the late 1980s, most of the male collective counseling groups within the men's movement had dissolved, which I think is related to the decline of autonomous radical feminism. Already in the 1980s there was an awareness of the potential for a kind of Jordan B. Peterson or "incel" type of regression as "male liberation" was initiated in response to feminism. We cannot really speak of an "inner drive." Toward the late 1980s, a lot of the autonomous and so-called "new social movements," in which the squatter movement played a central role in the Netherlands, started to fall apart (as described in Adilkno's *Cracking the Movement, Squatting Beyond the Media* [1994]).[9] In part, this was because the positions of these movements had become more mainstream, but also because they had not institutionalized themselves to the same degree as those of the 1968 generation.

SL: The *Bilwet Fascismemap* shows a clear basis in male feminism and male liberation, but what struck me was the somewhat absent matters of race and colonialism. It is brought up in the Tintin analyses, but overall seems to be lacking.[10] How do you look back at this now?

GL: That's a valid judgment. The squatter movement that I was part of in the 1980s was predominantly white, although we did have contacts with the organized left-wing Moroccan and Turkish workers.

At the time, we mostly interacted with Moroccan and Turkish migrants as organized groups, instead of how they are referred to now as "the Moroccans" or "the Turks." Although Moroccan and Turkish families were also squatting, we did not understand this as an outcome of racist housing policy. Surinamese and Antillean activist groups had squatted parts of the Bijlmer in 1975, but this did not become part of the predominantly white squatters' movement history.[11] We started to actively work with people and groups from these communities from 1985 onwards, but mostly via the production of media and Amsterdam's public access cable channel SALTO.

Dutch colonial history was not analyzed in any fundamental manner and put on the agenda at the time—at least not by us. The connection between the persistence of racism and the history of Dutch colonialism only became a matter of intense public debate much later—I would say in the past ten years. For my generation, colonialism was certainly on the agenda but with a focus on the anti-colonial struggles that dominated the decades after World War II. It was in this context that I got my political education. At 15, in 1975—the year of the independence of the Dutch colony of Suriname—I joined Third World Shop, a Christian-Marxist group where we read classics such as Frantz Fanon, Anton de Kom, and E.F. Schumacher. The work consisted of "remote" solidarity work with independence movements in Angola, Mozambique, Palestine, and Vietnam, of course.

The research on racism that we, as squatters, encountered in the early 1980s came to us primarily from the Anne Frank Foundation, since they were strong advocates for inquiry into race and colonialism in the Netherlands. However, the 1983 racist murder of a Dutch teenager of Netherlands Antillean descent, Kerwin Duinmeijer, was an enormous shock to us and became a major issue for the movement. We were focused on the "new right" as we encountered it back then, such as the Centrumpartij (Center Party) with Hans Janmaat, who can be considered one of the forerunners of such politicians as Pim Fortuyn, Geert Wilders, and now, Thierry Baudet.[12] The Centrumpartij did not have the elitist aspect that characterizes contemporary right-wing parties, and was in that sense more sub-proletarian and also more closely connected to violent forms of the extreme right in the Netherlands. Nowadays, Dutch right-wing parties have effectively outlawed their most violent expressions and have thereby been able to claim a substantial portion of the electoral pie.

Esmee Schoutens: Was there a specific reason to operate as a collective with Bilwet? And do you see a relationship with the rise of neoliberalism, privatization, and individualism during the 1980s and 1990s?

GL: We were not necessarily an anonymous collective; we mostly published under the group name but also used our first names with Bilwet as a surname—as in Geert Bilwet. The collective was part of an ecosystem of autonomous research initiatives such as SPOK, Kafka, Ultimatum, and Jansen & Janssen. There was a division of labor as these collectives all focused on different themes, such as neofascism or police infiltration. Bilwet focused on theory and the media. Retrospectively, we could also call it "autonomous cultural studies."

Being a member of a collective was also a question of privilege in some way; we were unemployed and on the dole, which made it possible for each of us to be involved in Bilwet on a full-time basis. There were no jobs anyway (they had all gone to the people now called "boomers"). Next to the writing we were intermittently also teaching, producing radio shows, and publishing *Arcade: Jaarboek voor Ambulante Wetenschappen* (Arcade: Annals of the Ambulatory Sciences, 1989–1995).[13]

As for privatization, I see a direct connection between the introduction of neoliberalism in the Netherlands after 1993–1994 and the rapid disintegration of all social movements and autonomous infrastructures. The arrival of neoliberalism in the Netherlands was not experienced as an ideology that was imported from the outside, from Reagan or Thatcher, but something that a lot of people actively supported as their own. We then also saw the rise of early elements of what are now called the creative industries, and a new form of entrepreneurial culture that became apparent in the Amsterdam club and rave scene, which started in the squatting scene but then quickly moved away from its roots.

ES: How does Bilwet's research on fascism feed into the development of the tactical media discourse? What characterizes this relationship?

GL: I believe there is no direct relationship between the two—unless you want to make a connection between our analysis of fascism and the transformation of that question into the media question. For many of the authors we read at the time, from

Virilio to Kittler, the media question is born out of the technologies of war. Whereas totalitarian systems are centered on the one voice of the leader, one nation, and one party, "Western" propaganda is technologically produced by a multiplicity of voices. Both are driven by desire, but in the totalitarian case, it channels toward the One, whereas in the Western models, desire is multiple and diverse.

After the publication of the first book by the Bilwet collective, *Het beeldenrijk* (The Empire of Images, 1985), the question of how to organize the media became so important—also in connection with the democratization of computers, video, radio, cable television, Xerox, etc.—that we had to shift our focus.[14] Moreover, our research and analysis of fascism became more of a question of memory and how memory is organized. We focused on the first history of the Amsterdam squatters' movement, *Cracking the Movement, Squatting Beyond the Media*, and on *The Media Archive* (1992), which really pushed us into the direction of new media (arts).[15] In this period, I was an editor of the video art magazine *Mediamatic* (1989–1994), and we simultaneously published similar short texts (called "Unidentified Theory Objects") in the Flemish film magazine *Andere Sinema* (Another Cinema). Similar to other collectives at the time, we wrote everything in Dutch. *Mediamatic* was the first opportunity for us to get our work out in English. I then also started to arrange German translations from 1991 onwards.

The XYZ of Tactical Media

ES: To go back to "The ABC of Tactical Media" manifesto and Next 5 Minutes, the tactical media conference series that you co-organized in the 1990s: How do you see the role of the "tactician" for which you have strongly advocated?[16]

> **GL:** The figure of the tactician is a response to the inability of those of my generation, but also of the generations before and after me, to establish themselves as a counterforce with the ability to scale up. The problem was never a lack of ideas, but in the end, we tacticians did not know how to properly gain in influence, and perhaps . . . power. We had, of course, a very different economic basis from, for instance, the labor unions, and we did not originate from the pillarization that characterized Dutch society during the twentieth century.

ES: At the same time, you celebrated the power of the low-budget and DIY.

> **GL:** It was a desperate attempt to continue to do something. In the 1990s, there was still a firm belief in the power of ideology, and the ideological battle was all about the development of powerful subversive or even seductive concepts. The tactician is a concept worker who builds a concept that can, in a Gramscian way, battle for the minds and hearts of the people. The meme is a similar, contemporary concept: you can do whatever you want with the meme but you cannot destroy its core, its architecture. The meme travels while its subversive core remains intact. We had similar ideas about the viral quality of "indy" media, which—besides tactical—we also called "sovereign." We saw our media as a strong time machine; an idea that was developed during a time when activists and artists realized they could not, or no longer, develop substantial counter-institutions.

SL: Twenty years later, Steve Bannon has appropriated this kind of reasoning, with the alt-right making use of a certain reductive and instrumental reading of Antonio Gramsci and his concept of hegemony. Bannon coupled memefied Gramscianism with algorithmic power.

GL: Exactly. The power of political memes also increases by buying Facebook ads, because content will not be distributed for free. Hence, Gramsci plus capital. When we think of the year 2016, we do not think of some kind of heroic battle between Fox News and CNN; it's Cambridge Analytica versus old-school television. Asymmetrical warfare, if you like: beat television ads with personalized Facebook ads. When we think of that time, in retrospect, we know that the mobilization of and huge investments in social media manipulation was the real battle-ground. In that sense, the real culture wars were by and large invisible, rather than consisting of the spectacular skirmishes that took place on these very same social media platforms—and we could only discover what was happening retrospectively. I believe there is much more going on in terms of "manipulated" content than "fake news" as old-school propaganda. The theoretical term "algorithmic governance" is too nice and harmless in this respect.

SL: The ultimate medium that constitutes the real battleground is the human brain.

GL: The human brain is the final frontier. The problem is that we are lacking an intermediate public interface that would enable us to find out what is going on. The publics are all highly personalized and individualized. In such a case, can one even talk about culture wars? There is a war happening over the hearts and minds of the people, there is no doubt. Yet this war is invisible, asymmetrical, and subconscious. Visible battlefronts matter less. This is a problem for both activists and artists, as we are all very focused on visible, audible, and written forms of power and prejudice. Politically correct behavior policing has no understanding of algorithmic forms of control—at least, not yet. The invisible culture wars on social media can be read as a response to the all-too-obvious old-school propaganda in the mainstream media that everyone can now easily "read" and shoot down as "ideology." But how do we read the ideology of Facebook and Google? Even in mainland China this is not so easy, although there the interventions of the Communist Party on Weibo, WeChat, Baidu, and Tencent are more clear cut. It took us quite some time to understand the reasons behind the strange recommendations we were seeing on YouTube.

SL: At The Society of Post-Control symposium, organized by Framer Framed (Amsterdam) in early 2017, after Trump had won the US presidency, there were quite a few veterans of the tactical media scene who asked themselves: How could the alt-right have appropriated tactical media, what the fuck happened, and were we asleep at the wheel?

GL: Now, three years later, there are more people from the tactical media scene who understand the alt-right's tactics, such as data mining and strategic communication. But in the Netherlands, we do not have regulatory mechanisms to prevent big tech companies from selling data and and thus cannot intervene in these manipulative practices. In Germany, the situation is slightly different in terms of privacy regulations, but in the Netherlands, the tech sector is left to the market, to its "natural" forces. We should not be surprised when artistic and activist techniques are appropriated by the market or the fascists. This is to be expected. The question is: What's to be done? What are the powerful concepts that we can use today? As I tried to explain in my recent work, over the past 30 years there has been a shift from media to network to platform centrality.[17] To experiment with tactics in the age of platform capitalism means recognizing that we are working under fundamentally different conditions.

ES: During the Next 5 Minutes 2 (N5M2) conference in 1996, there were already similar right-wing voices on the internet as there are today. What were your strategies or tactics to counter them back then? At N5M2 there was also a panel session dedicated to the role and importance of tactical research[18]; what were some of the key insights then, and what are their echoes now?

GL: There were various right-wing voices online at the time, resulting, for instance, in a big clash with the Church of Scientology from 1995 to 1997 about the online publication of secret writings. There were also Hindu nationalist groups in India on USENET. The network of people around N5M2 used several tactics such as DDoS (distributed denial-of-service) attacks and blocking servers, but also revealing the tactics of the opponent, infiltration, counter-infiltration, and leaking, which are still relevant today.

Activist (social) media research in general continues to this day, and in a broader sense, is also about creating an awareness of implicit forms of manipulation that aim to steer information dissemination, as Cambridge Analytica did. A good example is citizen involvement in the climate change debate, and especially in the research and interpretation of big data. Many people spend a lot of time on this because the question of how to read climate statistics is at the core of today's culture wars. Think of weather data or nitrogen levels: should we create our own data or engage in the fight over the interpretation of other people's data? The belief in the neutrality of scientists and experts has gone up in past decades, not down.

ES: During the 1990s you already warned of the escalation of "fake news" online, although it was not named as such. Many of these discussions were about reaching a point in the (near) future when people would not be able to determine anymore what is true and what is of value. To what extent did you see the "fake news" crisis of today coming?

GL: As tacticians we had two different terms to discuss this process. The first was "information overload," a concept which had already been developed in the 1970s. We experienced that ourselves in the mid-1990s and were well aware of its potential consequences. Then, as a countermeasure, we worked with what was one of the central concepts of Nettime: collaborative text filtering.[19] We envisioned this editing of each other's texts and writing theory together via e-mail as an answer to the growing indifference of the world toward the avalanche of "marginal" or niche internet content. But in doing so, we also already pointed out that it should be done by the communities concerned about this content themselves—because if they did not do it, others would do it for them.

This is precisely what we know Google and Facebook are now doing. They use automated machine learning to do collaborative text filtering for everyone because we do not do it ourselves anymore. We have conveniently outsourced it to their machines—along with all the consequences. At the same time, the vast majority of people celebrate this process because it is uniquely targeted to them and gives them the sense and pride that they are a unique person.

SL: This is an important point because it touches upon the privatization of culture, in the sense of a corporate-driven platform economy, but also of culture as a seemingly private realm, reduced to the individual who is targeted and manipulated on a micro-level. To overcome or escape this double privatization of culture, what could contemporary forms of collaborative filtering be? Could they be strengthened and made more public?

GL: Collaborative text filtering is still operational: think, for instance, of the content in your social media feed that is given to you by your network instead of the algorithm. What Nettime, Syndicate, Rohrpost, and other e-mail lists used to do in the past is what the sites like The Syllabus, Hacker News, and New Models are doing today: not just merely providing "alternative news" but alternatives to news as such. Social media platforms today are especially built for busy people who do not have much time. We skim the headlines; Google, Facebook, and Twitter all rely on the difficulty of our understanding and reconstructing the source of information, and deliberately and continuously blur the boundaries between trusted and questionable or fake sources. This contains the core of the big tech corporations' strategy, and it is also the reason why it is almost impossible to create new forms of public and progressive collaborative text filtering because we have to compete with machines at the highest level.

Requiems and Beyond

SL: You were never an internet utopian. With the notion of organized networks, or orgnets, for instance, you sought to intervene in actually existing network culture and take it beyond its (neo)liberal horizon.[20] The situation today has shifted to a platform economy, in which people think they are clicking buttons, but they are the buttons being clicked. To return to a passage in your "Requiem for the Network" essay, the design of social media platforms invites us "to respond to each and every event primarily and only with stripped-down opinions, basic responses."[21] Do you see media platforms' standardized protocols leading to certain forms of individuation and the contemporary notion of free speech and self-expression?

GL: Standardized protocols promote a certain culture of response, as exemplified by the fact that you can only "like" and not "dislike." As long as that is the case, there is a reduction. Countercultural media are not about individuals in this sense but about collectives and groups that can facilitate a platform for unique individuals who would not be heard otherwise. Of course, there is always a tension between the collective and the individual, but within this dialectical relationship it has almost become impossible to create movements.

SL: When we talk about movements that attack hegemonic forces, do we then assume that these are necessarily emancipatory or progressive movements? Or might such movements actually be profoundly troubling, reactionary, proto-fascist, or formless, and risk going off into a different direction? I think the question should be: Is it impossible in these circumstances to create *progressive* counter-movements?

> **GL:** In the Netherlands, one experiences misery and boredom about the impossibility of setting up new movements, but this is not a reflection of the global situation. It is a local feeling. And even in the Netherlands, we do still protest, if you look at demonstrations around health care and education, for instance. Last year, there were thousands of people on the streets against climate devastation, and Dutch farmers occupied highways against a possible reduction of livestock. In the 1930s, both reactionary and progressive movements were present, and literally clashed in the streets. When we talk about organization, we talk about the organization question on both sides—and appropriation also happens on both sides: of technologies and techniques, motives and memes, fashions and social media tricks.

ES: In relation to the tactical media scene of the 1990s you have stressed the coming together or assembling of collectives and groups in physical places, such as printing houses or media centers. What is the role of physical gatherings, or "meetspaces," today? 22

> **GL:** When we look at contemporary movements, a lot of the preparation seems to be happening online. There are manifestations happening but usually in larger, centralized spaces. It is increasingly difficult to operate in multiple smaller, decentralized spaces; in most cases, these have either vanished due to processes of gentrification or were pushed to the

margins of the city where they are less visible. That does not mean that these spaces have been eradicated but that there are fewer of them. I do not believe in purely virtual movements. People will invest whatever it takes to come together in real life. "Meetspace," by the way, is a play on "meatspace," the place where human bodies, or "wetware" as we also called it in the early 1990s, gather—surely a reference to the line "what a piece of meat" in The Stranglers' song "Princess of the Streets" from 1979.[23] Meeting-in-real-life holds this promise of "hot" sexual encounters, unlike "cold" and rational computational exchanges.

SL: Your writings from the 1990s and early 2000s about meetspace and temporary media labs are still relevant, for instance, in certain cultural and artistic milieus that employ the method of the workshop or training session. At the same time, a figure such as Bannon also actively uses meetspaces, like the school he unsuccessfully attempted to establish at a monastery in Italy, to bring people together temporarily. The meetspace, too, is open for (re)appropriation from several sides—and in 2020, the question has rapidly become how to salvage at least part of it in a culture of social distancing and permanent Zoom conferences. How can one reinvent or rearticulate the dialectic of networked communication and physical meeting for the present, specifically for emancipatory forms of practice and organizational modes, and in post-Covid-19 society?

GL: When we talk about platform politics, there is, on the one hand, a regulatory school, and on the other, a school that promotes creating one's own platforms. Not just as marginal infrastructures, but as public infrastructures. Think, for example, of utilities or large co-ops with a clear dedication to the commons. We need to think in larger infrastructures that involve many people, not individual solutions.

SL: I am with you when it comes to the importance of commonist organizational politics. However, couldn't it lead to a problematic split between progressive organizational politics—and organizational aesthetics, or organizational art—on the one hand, and the fascist targeting and re-making of subjects, on the other? That is to say: while we are playing around with organizing relations and practicing differently, the Bannons, Trumps, Baudets, and Kubitscheks are actually reprogramming minds on a large scale, with dramatic consequences.

GL: Precisely, and there is the risk that the arts—with its small and confined spaces—become an infrastructure that is no longer in contact with any of the concerns in wider society. There are many places one can think of that need to be occupied, but the museum is not on the list. The real fight is happening over infrastructure. From a content perspective, the media is culture and ideology, but the media is also an infrastructure of networks and platforms, an infrastructure that people can or cannot have access to, can or cannot shape, can or cannot own, and so on. Since the 1990s, one can see a growing indifference toward the content of the media. As opposed to the political engagement with the media's content in the 1970s and 1980s, there is a growing tendency to just surf the surface, to stay at the interface. This can be extended to the motive of the brain as medium and final frontier as we discussed earlier.

SL: Infrastructures are both technical and institutional—even though we tend to think of some of them, such as social media platforms, as being primarily technical and others, such as universities and museums, as primarily institutional. I think in both cases the real question is what used to be called the *Organisationsfrage* in 1960s German leftist circles. We are still struggling with the organizational question today—and we seem to keep oscillating between various options, bouncing back and forth. One can attempt the "long march through the institutions," in Rudi Dutschke's famous phrase, which still suggests one has a hope of changing existing institutions; or one can try to *undercommon* them. Alternatively, one can try to build autonomous organizations from the ground up, or graft them onto existing structures, as you have done with your para-institution here at the Amsterdam University of Applied Sciences, the Institute of Network Cultures. Do we indeed need all these tactics in parallel, in order to learn what works under specific circumstances?

GL: The labor movement was powerful until it was crushed by Nazism, discredited by Stalinism, co-opted by the Western welfare state, and then killed by neoliberalism. As an institutional counterforce it had a very strong infrastructure. Post-World War II social movements have not really been able to build such an infrastructure, and, indeed, the march through the institutions was one idea that came out of the 1960s student movement—which means that you do not build the institutions yourself, but you take over the ones that already exist. There is an element of laziness in this. A good example is education. Here in the Netherlands, we no longer start our own schools or universities, think tanks or research centers, but we should. There are some self-organized initiatives but not too many. Some of them have grown out of the journalism crisis, such as Follow the Money, *De Correspondent*, the Panama Papers coalition, Bellingcat, and Forensic Architecture. I still emphasize that we need autonomous units, free spaces, inside or outside larger institutions. We have to organize ourselves beyond the virtual, because I do not believe in the benevolence of individuals in high-ranking positions. It's not their job to change the status quo. They are not accountable and should be ignored. For too long we have looked at (celebrity) individuals in leadership positions instead of looking at our own potential to organize counterpower.

1 Bilwet is an acronym standing for the Stichting ter Bevordering van Illegale Wetenschap; the equivalent English acronym Adilkno stands for the Foundation for the Advancement of Illegal Knowledge.

2 David Garcia and Geert Lovink, "The ABC of Tactical Media," *Nettime*, 16 May 1997, https://www.nettime.org/Lists-Archives/nettime-l-9705/msg00096.html.

3 The Society of Post-Control symposium, Framer Framed, Amsterdam, 22 January 2017.

4 Geert Lovink, "Requiem for the Network," in *The Eternal Network: The Ends and Becomings of Network Culture*, Kristoffer Gansing and Inga Luchs, eds. (Amsterdam and Berlin: Institute of Network Cultures and transmediale e.V., 2020), p. 106.

5 Geert Lovink and Bas-Jan van Stam, "De gewonnen, de verloren, de permanente oorlog," in *Bilwet Fascismemap (1983–1994)*, ed. Sepp Eckenhaussen, (1984; repr., Amsterdam: Institute of Network Cultures, 2019), pp. 109–134, https://networkcultures.org/blog/publication/bilwet-fascismemap-1983-1994.

6 Ibid., p. 130.

7 Sepp Eckenhaussen, ed., *Bilwet Fascismemap (1983–1994)* (Amsterdam: Institute of Network Cultures, 2019).

8 Klaus Theweleit, *Männerphantasien, Bd. 1: Frauen, Fluten, Körper, Geschichte* (Reinbek: Rowohlt, 1983).

9 Adilkno, *Cracking the Movement, Squatting Beyond the Media*, trans. Laura Martz (Brooklyn: Autonomedia, 1994).

10 See the section "Kuifosofie en Datadandy" (Tintinology and Datadandy), in *Bilwet Fascismemap*, ed. Sepp Eckenhaussen (Amsterdam: Institute of Network Cultures, 2019), pp. 248–287.

11 The Bijmermeer or Bijlmer is an area in the Southeast of Amsterdam, known for its postwar housing projects.

12 An important publication that could be mentioned in this context is *De rechterkant van Nederland: Een overzicht van extreemrechtse en fascistische verschijnselen in Nederland* (Amsterdam: SUA, 1983), by a loose group of friends that were close to Bilwet.

13 *Arcade: Jaarboek voor Ambulante Wetenschappen* (Amsterdam: Ravijn, editions published 1989, 1990, 1991, 1993, and 1995).

14 Bilwet, *Het beeldenrijk: Over stralingsangst en ruimteverlangen* (Amsterdam: Raket en Lont, 1985).

15 Adilkno, *The Media Archive*, trans. Laura Martz (Brooklyn: Autonomedia, 1998).

16 In total, four editions of the Next 5 Minutes conference took place, in 1993, 1996, 1999, and 2001. Lovink co-organized Next 5 Minutes with, among others, David Garcia, Caroline Nevejan, Menno Grootveld, Bas Raijmakers, Geke van Dijk, Marleen Stikker, Andreas Broeckmann, and Erik Kluitenberg.

17 See, in particular, "Requiem for the Network," in *The Eternal Network*, pp. 102–115.

18 The session at Next 5 Minutes 2 was titled "Tactical Research – The Myth of Easy Search," de Balie, Amsterdam, 20 January 1996, and included presentations by Frannie Armstrong, Jamie Hartzell, Christian Golla, and Babeth, moderated by Eveline Lubbers (of the research collective Jansen & Janssen).

19 Nettime is a "collaborative editing" listserv focused on network discussions and net criticism that was founded in 1995 by an interdisciplinary group of people working in digital media art, theory, and activism, among them Lovink.

20 See Geert Lovink and Ned Rossiter, *Organization After Social Media* (Colchester: Minor Compositions, 2018).

21 Lovink, "Requiem for the Network," p. 106.

22 Geert Lovink, "The Importance of Meetspace: On Conferences and Temporary Media Labs," in *Dark Fiber: Tracking Critical Internet Culture* (Cambridge, MA: MIT Press, 2002), pp. 240–253; first published on Nettime as "The Importance of Meetspace: A Manual for Temporary Media Labs," Nettime, 8 January 2000, https://nettime.org/Lists-Archives/nettimel-0001/msg00041.html.

23 Geert Lovink and Rik Delhaas, eds., *Wetware* (Amsterdam: Uitgeverij De Balie, 1991).

Deep Bureaucracy and Autonomist AI

Dan McQuillan

Artificial intelligence (AI) is here at last. But what exactly is it, and what is it going to change? The AI emerging from Silicon Valley and Beijing is certainly uncanny, but it doesn't meet the expectations created by the movies. It's heralded as the birth of near-human intelligence but seems to be warping social relations wherever it appears, whether in social media or new structures of precarious employment. Given the global rise in reactionary politics, the future arriving at the same moment that the far-right past has returned should provoke skepticism. While talking heads focus on some imagined superintelligence, actually existing AI is rolling over marginalized communities in the here and now. An AI future seems nonnegotiable, but the nature of neoliberalism and the legacy of colonialism should already warn against a destiny driven by deep learning. I'm suggesting that AI is an intensification of what's gone before rather than any kind of quantum leap, specifically, as an intensification of bureaucracy and the derivatives market. Doubling down on distributed manipulation is a political move that brings specific harms in the form of segregation and automated scarcity, so I also propose a standpoint and a set of tactics that push for an alter-AI: that is, for an approach that recomposes AI according to an alternative vision of togetherness.

Welfare Bureaucracy

At first glance, bureaucracy and AI don't seem to have that much in common. Bureaucracy is the gray zone of organizational administration that relies on boring forms and procedures, while AI is the cutting-edge computational technology whose intelligence may be about to outstrip that of human beings. But rather than the bridge to an alternative sci-fi future, AI can be understood as an upgrade to the existing bureaucratic order, that is, as an iteration of the logic that unifies governments and corporations. This actual AI is not a filmic fantasy but applied machine learning of various kinds, including artificial neural networks and deep learning. Bureaucracy, according to its biographer Max Weber, emerged as a mechanism for the state to impose control and rationality on increasingly complex societies. AI is part of the same quest for traction in a turbulent world. Exactly like bureaucracy, AI is a mode of goal-oriented rational ordering that claims neutrality and objectivity through detached abstraction.

The functionaries who are already effecting this transformation do not see their work as the state administration of a Terminator-like intelligence. Rather, a shift to AI governmentality makes sense in terms of the perceived virtues of bureaucracy: as a moral comportment that is evidence-driven and rational, one that cultivates a wariness toward emotional entanglement and valorizes indifference as the means to effective implementation of policy. There is, of course, a growing awareness that AI's uncanny powers seem to be stained by bias, because however clever the computers become, they are learning from data generated by people living their messy and prejudiced lives. But public administrations already operate under these conditions. Indeed, the virtue of bureaucracy is seen as limiting the effect of any partiality among its professionals through technocracy and rigid rules. The wave of research by the machine-learning community into de-biasing datasets exactly complements the bureaucratic mindset through its technocratic solutionism and the formal audits taken as sufficient guarantors of balance.

The distortions that cannot be undone are the architectural ones that unite both bureaucracy and AI: the reliance on distance and abstraction. Bureaucracy achieves its authority by abstracting from the detail of the social world to apply policy at sufficient scale to make modern governmentality possible. It is foundational to bureaucracy to extend "the distance at which human action is able to bring effect."[1] Machine learning begins with data points that are already a set of quantified abstractions from some target context. It constructs a loss function that represents in some abstract sense the sum of distances in a high-dimensional feature space between data points and the predictions of the algorithm. The "learning" in "machine learning" comes from computational optimization that iteratively minimizes this loss function. The resulting parameters are the model that can be used for classification and prediction. These architectures of abstraction and the leveraging of distance—of institutional form and algorithmic computation—are becoming fused through the force of financial crisis. AI is seen as a key solution to the challenges of austerity, where every state actor is required to do more with less. Under the cover of crisis, the technocrats of administration and the technocrats of computing are collaborating on operations of abstraction, distance, and optimization, both insulated by a reliance on technical morality.

Thus, the impact of actual AI—that is, how machine learning is applied in the world—is shifting from the white noise of social networks to the transformation of state functions. Applying algorithms to welfare payments, for example, is presented as a benign upgrade of a bloated system; an entirely administrative matter that needs no democratic debate, let alone community co-design. While many of the current welfare state algorithms are clumsy codifications of existing bureaucratic assumptions, they are already being adopted for areas such as child protection and healthcare. Machine learning systems are the next step in this extant but largely invisible shift to algorithms in public services. In Sweden, algorithms have been issuing warnings and withholding benefit payments; in Spain, they've been discarding applications from poor households for electricity subsidies; and in Austria, they've been scoring job seekers to decide whether or not they get help, and doing so in a way that discriminates against women and disabled people.

In the name of efficiency and narrowing the pool of benefits claimants, new and intrusive forms of conditionality are introduced. While the overt reason is mostly austerity, the process is also being exploited for social reengineering by algorithms: that is, as a kind of automation shock doctrine. Recent reports by the UN's Special Rapporteur on extreme poverty and human rights describe myriad ways in which digital transformation and the shift to algorithmic governance conceals significant alterations to the political-structural landscape. In the Netherlands, an algorithm called SyRI (Systeem Risico Indicatie, or System Risk Indication) tapped into a large array of government databases to draw up lists of people suspected of housing or benefits fraud by calculating their similarity to data profiles of previous fraudulent claims. High water consumption, for example, may have been seen as an indicator that someone receiving a single person's benefit was cohabiting with someone else. In a micro-demonstration of policy-by-data-science, SyRI has only been applied to specific neighborhoods with high levels of poverty and deprivation, and, when the algorithm is applied, the data analyst sets parameters that define the local "risk range." The fashionable liberal focus on algorithmic ethics diverts attention from this increasingly widespread substitution of technical operations for democratic discourse.

Derivatives

Bureaucracies are already not what they used to be. Under neoliberalism they have been increasingly transformed into arms-length agencies with entrepreneurial goals, where senior bureaucrats don't implement policies but design a market of incentives and penalties intended to optimize contractual outcomes from outsourced services. Adding AI will take this marketization to a new level by mobilizing quantifications of risk as a form of derivative. Public institutions pervaded by artificial neural networks will become futures exchanges for bundles of citizen risk factors. The way that neural networks will so intensively financialize administration and governance is related to their internal operations. When training a deep learning algorithm, diverse features of the world are normalized to numbers between zero and one such that they can be traded against each other in an iterative process called gradient descent. You don't need to tell neural networks what features to use; you just force enough labeled data forward through the layers, then pass the errors backward to optimize the fit. Neural networks can handle the messy patterns that defeat other algorithms. It's neural networks that make facial recognition possible and power the conversational abilities of personal assistants like Alexa and Siri. This leads to a kind of hubris among practitioners, a belief that, given a sufficiently large dataset and a target to optimize on, they can derive a model that will solve pretty much any problem. But this process of hyper-abstracting the diversity of the world's materiality into planes of numerical consistency that can be mathematically manipulated and traded is also the dark pattern behind derivatives.

Derivatives are, of course, the financial products that have come to dominate international markets. Their value is derived from an underlying asset or group of assets and varies according to their fluctuations. They are ways of dealing with risk by taking positions on likely future values. One particular form of derivative is the Collateralized Debt Obligation (CDO), a complex structure that bundles together loans and other assets. Subprime mortgage-backed securities become the source of huge inflation in the market for CDOs and it was the bursting of that bubble that triggered the financial crisis of 2007–2008. Perhaps surprisingly, derivatives, including CDOs, are still the dynamo of world markets. This same logic is now migrating directly into social life via new forms of algorithmic risk assessment based on data, not about industries or capital assets but about everyday lives and behaviors. These social-behavioral assets are not being bet on by financial traders but are being quantified and optimized by institutions in making decisions about their matters of concern, whether it's a large company calculating which employee is the most likely to leave or social services calculating which parents are most likely to abuse their children. Like futures markets, AI models the probabilities of particular outcomes, projecting values into likelihoods that are then treated as more real than the actualities that they supposedly represent.

The obsession with accuracy metrics so visible in the machine learning profession shouldn't be misunderstood as an attempt to asymptotically approach a reliable representation of reality. This isn't science but the construction of data derivatives, an operation of stabilization that recomposes abstracted risk characteristics into commensurable bundles. The confident promoters of AI solutionism don't consider whether decisions based on the complexity of leveraged calculations will introduce new forms of instability or have unintended consequences. Prediction-oriented risk assessments introduce a feedback loop of iterative amplification because they can't account for their own interventions in the system. Recent history offers lessons here. Many scholars see risk assessment as the key historical driver in the massive growth and racial disparities of the United States prison population, through the knock-on effects it had on people's lives. Incarceration means weakened familty ties, reduced employment opportunties, and ratcheting up of recidivism. Hence "risk profiling" increases risk. The social effects of AI are further deepened through segregation and a reduction of dignity.

Segregation and Dignity

When AI applies its optimized model to input data, it makes predictions by discriminating between one target class and another. In neural networks the final layers are designed to force an outcome from the non-linearity of the neurons' activations so that the output classifications act like probabilities, that is, they are all values between zero and one and together sum to a total of one. The predicted label is the class with the highest probability. There will always be a predicted output, however poor the correlations, which explains the certainty with which a neural network will pick a result even when presented with deliberately misleading input data. The way AI arrives at its classifications is by calculating distances: by determining some abstract metric of difference as a distance. The basis of machine learning is a constructed homophily, a forcing of closeness in data space. But treating an abstract distance in data space as an innate affinity is the logic of statistical segregation. As media theorist Wendy Hui Kyong Chun points out, racism can also be seen as a technology of segregation.[2] Race itself is a kind of tool, as the sociologist Ruha Benjamin writes, "one designed to stratify and sanctify social injustice as part of the architecture of everyday life," and AI constructs the world in the same way.[3] The relationship of AI to racism won't be fully dispersed by more inclusive training data; it's more fundamental. AI systems will automate discrimination not simply because they are being adopted in already racist societies but because their core technical operations work that way.

Of course, labeling and classification are mundane methods used in filtering through daily reality, but raised to institutional principles for the distribution of goods and harms, they have always reinforced asymmetries of power. Inflated credibility will be given to machinic assessments over the already suspect voice of the service user. Whether you're a recipient of benefit payments or a precariously employed Uber driver, your status is not as a rights holder but as a supplicant to an algorithm. It's a minimization not just of the loss function but of dignity. The resultant ranking of the deserving and the undeserving becomes a calculative Victorianism, assigning morality via statistical metrics. The social logic of derivatives induced by algorithms and pervasive risk scoring produces new forms of debt, not only the kind of monetary debt miscalculated by the so-called "robo-debt" algorithm in Australia, but a debt that is the inverse of "social credit," an algorithmic negative that cuts off access to services. A recent Airbnb patent uses machine learning to use credit checks and crawls of social media accounts in combination to infer whether a client displays the untrustworthy traits of "narcissism, Machiavellianism, or psychopathy."[4] Meanwhile, socially marginalized groups are reporting increased exclusion from the service.

The Targeted Compliance Framework in Australia creates a "mutual obligation" for claimants to update a digital dashboard with their job-seeking activities and to check their compliance status. Any slip in this self-monitoring leads to a suspension of payments even though many users lack digital literacy or find that the automated system fails to take real-life situations into account. The algorithmic gaze is used to select points of inconsistency that can be leveraged against those who are already vulnerable, extending control over an increasing raft of behavioral details in much the same way as the smallest deviation of a worker in an Amazon warehouse can degrade their work credit leading to automated severance. Algorithmic governance increases the blurring between state and corporation in enacting social control over the least powerful in the same way that austerity and precarity have erased the boundary between employment and poverty. The mathematics of AI seem abstract, but ideologically charged terms such as efficiency, targeting, and minimization slide freely between political rhetoric and machine learning. The classifications operationalized by AI are performative. Decision boundaries won't remain mathematical constructs but will determine the distribution of services and sanctions. Clashes of classification will operate across the spectrum of all who are already pushed toward marginal positions and each example will bring its own collateral damage. The only accountability will be economic, led by considerations of financial efficiency, as the accuracy figures of algorithms fuse with cost-related performance targets.

As machinic classifications are integrated into institutions, and as algorithmic bureaucracies infer people's membership of narrow categories in order to get their needs met, they multiply moments of administrative violence, especially for those who are already the most datafied. The mathematic morality of AI is not only a mechanism of post-austerity but a potential tool for social reengineering. This is not exactly an alien concept in Silicon Valley itself, the heartland of AI, where strong strains of elitism overlap with skepticism of a pluralist social order and leanings toward corporatist authoritarianism, based on assumptions about natural hierarchies of intelligence. Ultimately, the algorithmic coupling of vectorial distances and social differences can become the targeting of those who are claimed to be polluting national purity. The endpoint of an automated welfare state that is purely aligned with a national mission of economic success is to optimize out the "useless eaters." For those many thousand disabled people in the United Kingdom, for example, who have been reclassified as "fit for work," the administrative violence of such efficiencies then, very sadly, often becomes self-directed, as can be seen from the statistics on suicides.[5] It's not just "automating inequality" to apply data-driven force to the poorest; any logic that begins with the most vulnerable demographics in the great task of optimizing the whole populace is a fascist one.

Matters of Care

How can political action best contest a neural network new order? A good starting point is to treat AI not as a matter of intelligence but as a matter of care. By "care" I mean the invisibilized labor that is an inevitable consequence of social interdependence and which is usually gendered, racialized, and devalued. Care exists in the shadow of the kind of detachment and abstraction that is valorized by AI and yet it is the tangle of tasks without which people's lives would not work. A politics of care starts with concern about the exclusions and boundaries of a stratified society. The first question for any AI should not be how many marginal accuracy points it has gained on an accuracy benchmark, but how its reordering will increase present asymmetry in the burden of care. It is indeed ironic that AI's intensification of segregation is itself built on the hidden labor of clickworkers in the Global South, often women of color, who are labeling the necessary datasets.

Opposing this new order requires ways of knowing that can challenge the erasure of lived experience by the ideology of efficiency, and generate a counter project to the algorithmic production of carelessness. Treating AI as a matter of care is not only about concern for those who might be harmed but about the character of its core processes. The form of knowing enacted by AI depends on a separation between representations, the weights in the models, and that which they claim to represent. But the way AI acts in the world is such that subjects are actually produced and performed by these very same structures of knowing, invalidating the models as statistical insights but making them very effective as forms of subjection. Moving beyond the injustices enabled by data systems means moving beyond representation to social recomposition.

This isn't about machines versus people but about the way specific configurations of the technosocial can corrode sociality and mutual aid. Instead of asking for a more efficient way to model reality, it is better to concentrate on enacting a different world. AI is a form of apparatus in the sense that feminist theorist Karan Barad articulated; it produces at an ontological level the world it is designed to measure. Altering AI in practice would redraw the exclusions that produce phenomena and experience: that is, reclaiming agency through agential realism where discourse is not a matter of language but of changing the constraints on what can emerge. AI is a discursive apparatus whose role in sedimenting reality requires participatory reworking. Rather than iterative assimilation into the new order, the task at hand is to develop forms of participation that are lines of flight.

Workers' and People's Councils

One way to start this recomposition of AI is through people's councils. People's councils are bottom-up, federated structures that act as direct democratic assemblies, a model that goes back to the face-to-face democracy of the Athenian *ekklesia* (popular assemblies) but reemerges again and again in historical moments as a self-organized alternative to authoritarianism. Such assemblies are horizontal structures in which everyone has an equal say about the matter being decided. They are structures that deliberately reverse states of exclusion and exception, and act as counterweights to bureaucratic distance and abstraction. People's councils would interrupt statist AI with the situated perspectives of the ignored, promoting inclusion over efficiency and regenerating relationality so as to restructure common ways of knowing. Algorithmic bureaucracy constitutes one of the highest historical forms of the abstraction of social organization and needs to be counterbalanced by the unmediated relationships of popular assemblies. This is not a reconfiguring of representative democracy. People's councils are not representative because they challenge the validity of representation, but they are transformative because they are constitutive of a different commonality.

The alteration of AI also requires workers' councils. While neoclassical economics tries to construct liberal democracy as a common rationality of growth and prosperity for all, it foundationally excludes the workplace from the democratic sphere. Attempts by workers in AI to hold their employers to account run head on into this central contradiction. Workers' councils are the means by which AI workers can develop a vision as powerful as the transhumanist hubris of their parent corporations. Instead of being devalued as data and traded as risk factors, the objective must be to develop the creative and imaginative activities that constitute self-valorization, that is, the autonomous reinvention of conditions in the here and now. Contemporary tech worker dissent will become transformative when it sees itself as creating the possibility for a new society within the shell of the old. In this mode of change, acting at "scale" doesn't mean the exponential computation of machine learning models or the instrumentalist graph structures of social networks but of a democratic federation of councils.

AI is not coming to steal workers' jobs; it's coming to erase any distinction between work and precarious dependency. The conditions of precarious labor will be governed by the same logic of optimization as the weaponized welfare system. Only a form of self-organization that refuses this logic has any prospect of pushing back. The potential of council organization for both community life and economic activity has been put into practice in the autonomous zone of Rojava in north eastern Syria, under the auspices of democratic confederalism. This confederalism is based on the principle that all groups in society find expression through local meetings, general conventions, and councils. One of the most striking aspects has been the self-organization of women in this system, both within autonomous structures and through joint leadership of administrative and economic councils at all levels of the federal system. The council form is the anti-derivative; lived reality is addressed as a whole not through deconstruction, and incommensurability is overcome by consensus not stabilized quantification. This is the basis for an alter-AI, one that gains traction by starting from existing points of struggle at the margins: struggles over disability, welfare, housing, climate change, and immigration. It is not enough to reform the performance of hyper-abstracted optimization—it needs to be destroyed.

Deserting AI

What needs deserting is AI realism—the sense that an AI-driven future is inevitable. An AI-driven future will mean every aspect of life being traded as some kind of quantified risk. The new order isn't being announced in a press release from Silicon Valley or debated in parliaments but is being infrastructured through a reinvention of mundane state functions. AI is political, and the challenge to algorithmic stratification will come through political organization as much as a commitment to ethics and fairness. Neoliberalism itself was a line of flight from increased worker and community power, and it is the recomposition of those same struggles that can rein in its computational intensification. A reliance on abstraction and generalizability is not a route to superhuman powers, but a sign of vulnerability, a fear of being called to account by those presently carrying the burden of care. The way forward for a recomposed AI is not predictive but prefigurative. The aim must be to seek algorithmic operations that abandon their service to detachment and contribute instead to the reconstruction of the commons through militant caring.

1 Zygmunt Bauman, *Modernity and the Holocaust* (New York: Cornell University Press, 1989), cited in Paul du Gay, *In Praise of Bureaucracy* (Copenhagen: SAGE Publications Ltd, 2000), p. 36.

2 Wendy Hui Kyong Chun, "Introduction: Race and/as Technology; or, How to Do Things to Race," *Camera Obscura: Feminism, Culture, and Media Studies* 70, vol. 24, no.1 (2009), pp. 7–35, https://doi.org/10.1215/02705346-2008-013.

3 Ruha Benjamin, *Race After Technology: Abolitionist Tools for the New Jim Code* (Medford, MA: Polity Press, 2019), p. 17.

4 Sarabjit Singh Baveja, Anish Das Sarma, and Nilesh Dalvi. Determining trustworthiness and compatibility of a person. United States Patent 10169708, filed 28 December 2015, and issued 1 January 2019.

5 Ben Barr, David Taylor-Robinson, Alex Scott-Samuel, Martin McKee, and David Stuckler, *Suicides Associated with the 2008–10 Economic Recession in England: Time Trend Analysis* (BMJ, 2012), https://doi.org/10.1136/bmj.e5142.

Contributors

Bini Adamczak is an artist, social theorist, and writer whose practice explores political theory, queer feminism, and the past and future of revolutions. She is the author of *Communism for Kids* (2017), a story-book on, capitalism, crisis, and *Yesterday's Tomorrow: On the Loneliness of Communist Spectres and the Reconstruction of the Future* (2020), in which she discusses the history of Stalinism. Recent publications include *Der schönste Tag im Leben des Alexander Berkman. Vom möglichen Gelingen der Russischen Revolution* (2017); and *Beziehungsweise Revolution. 1917, 1968 und kommende* (2017). Adamczak lives in Berlin.

Kader Attia is an artist who explores the wide-ranging effects of Western cultural hegemony and colonialism. He has thematically focused on the notion of "repair." In 2016, Attia founded ~~La Colonie~~, a space in Paris for sharing ideas on decolonialization, not only of peoples but also of knowledge, attitudes, and practices. Among his recent exhibitions are *When Home Won't Let You Stay: Migration Through Contemporary Art*, Minneapolis Institute of Art, Minneapolis, 2020; *Kader Attia, The Museum of Emotion*, Hayward Gallery, London, 2019; and *Kader Attia, Roots Also Grow in Concrete*, Culturgest Fundação Caixa Geral de Depòsitos, Lisbon, 2018. Attia lives and works in Berlin and Algiers.

Rose Hammer is an artistic persona consisting of twenty artists that was created as a response to an invitation from osloBIENNALEN First Edition (2019–2024) to create a work in public space. Rose Hammer aims to escape the logic of the individual artist, becoming instead a transnational, transgenerational, and transdisciplinary persona. The group carefully considers relatively unknown stories at the origin of mainstream notions of identity, nationality, and history in order to construct a counternarrative, and to present it following the rules of Brechtian agitprop: with explicit, clearly formulated political positions, non-hierarchical dynamics, and a *reductio ad absurdum* of notions such as professionalism, virtuosity, and entertainment.

Maria Hlavajova is founding General and Artistic Director of BAK, basis voor actuele kunst, Utrecht, since 2000. In 2008–2016 she was Research and Artistic Director of the collaborative project FORMER WEST, which culminated in the publication *Former West: Art and the Contemporary After 1989* (co-edited with Simon Sheikh, 2016). Hlavajova has instigated and (co-)organized numerous projects at BAK and beyond, including the series *Propositions for Non-Fascist Living* (2017–ongoing), *Future Vocabularies* (2014–2017), and *New World Academy* (with artist Jonas Staal, 2013–2016), among many other international (research) projects. Her curatorial work includes *Call the Witness*, Roma Pavilion, 54th Venice Biennale, 2011; and *Citizens and Subjects*, Dutch Pavilion, 52nd Venice Biennale, Venice, 2007. In addition, Hlavajova is co-founder (with Kathrin Rhomberg) of the tranzit network. Hlavajova lives and works in Amsterdam and Utrecht.

Tom Holert is an art historian, writer, curator, and artist, and honorary professor of art theory and cultural studies at the Academy of Fine Arts Vienna. His research focuses on questions of art and knowledge politics, and the genealogies of contemporary art's ventures into knowledge production and pedagogy. In 2015, Holert (co-) founded the Harun Farocki Institut (HaFI) in Berlin. Holert curated the research and exhibition projects *Neolithic Childhood: Art in a False Present, c. 1930*, Haus der Kulturen der Welt, Berlin, 2018; and *Learning Laboratories: Architecture, Instructional Technology, and the Social*

Production of Pedagogical Space Around 1970, BAK, basis voor actuele kunst, Utrecht, 2016–2017. Recent publications include *Knowledge Beside Itself. Contemporary Art's Epistemic Politics* (2020). Holert lives and works in Berlin.

Geert Lovink is a media theorist, net critic, and activist. Lovink's recent projects focus on digital publishing and the future of art criticism. In 2004, Lovink founded the Institute of Network Cultures at the Amsterdam University of Applied Sciences, a center that analyzes and shapes the terrain of network cultures through events, publications, and online dialogue. Lovink is a member of Adilkno, and a former editor of the media art magazine *Mediamatic* (1989–1994). Publications include *Sad by Design: On Platform Nihilism* (2019), *Social Media Abyss: Critical Internet Cultures and the Force of Negation* (2016), *Networks Without a Cause: A Critique on Social Media* (2012), and *Zero Comments: Blogging and Critical Internet Culture* (2007). Lovink lives and works in Amsterdam.

Sven Lütticken is an art historian, critic, and editor. He teaches at Vrije Universiteit Amsterdam, and has written extensively on the central role of historical theory in contemporary art and media. He is a regular contributor to international journals and art magazines such as *New Left Review*, *Texte zur Kunst*, *Grey Room*, *e-flux journal*, and *Afterall*. Publications include the edited volumes *Art and Autonomy* (2019) and *Futurity Report* (with Eric de Bruyn, 2019), and the books *Cultural Revolution: Aesthetic Practice After Autonomy* (2017), *History in Motion: Time in the Age of the Moving Image* (2013), and *Idols of the Market: Modern Iconoclasm and the Fundamentalist Spectacle* (2009). Curated exhibitions include *The Strange Case of the Case*, Dutch Art Institute, Arnhem, 2017; *The Art of Iconoclasm*, BAK, basis voor actuele kunst, Utrecht, 2009; and *Life, Once*

More, Forms of Reenactment in Contemporary Art, Witte de With Center for Contemporary Art, Rotterdam, 2005. Lütticken lives and works in Utrecht.

Diana McCarty is an independent media producer and feminist media activist. Her work revolves around art, gender, politics, radical feminism, technology, and media. McCarty is a co-founder of reboot.fm, the award winning free artists' radio in Berlin, the cultural radio networks Radia Network (radia.fm), and of the FACES (faces-l) online community for women, among other initiatives. She co-initiated the exhibition *Nervous Systems: Quantified Life and the Social Question*, Haus der Kulturen der Welt, Berlin, 2016, and actively collaborates with the experimental media project *Luta ca caba inda*. As a cyberpunk in the 1990s, she was active in independent internet culture with nettime, the MetaForum conference series, and different hacking spaces. She was a 2019/2020 Fellow at BAK, basis voor actuele kunst, Utrecht. McCarty is a proud Chicana from Albuquerque, New Mexico. McCarty lives and works in Berlin.

Dan McQuillan is a researcher, computer scientist, and activist. With a background in experimental particle physics, he now teaches Creative and Social Computing at Goldsmiths, University of London, having previously worked as Amnesty International's director of e-communications. He is the founder of *Multikulti*, a community-led multilingual website for asylum seekers and refugees, and co-founder of Social Innovation Camp, which brought together ideas, people, and digital tools to prototype solutions to social problems. More recently, he co-founded Science for Change Kosovo, a youth-led citizen science project based on critical pedagogy and focused on the issue of air quality. As an activist, he was heavily involved in the G8 protest in Genoa in 2001. Recent publications include

People's Councils for Ethical Machine Learning (2018), *Data Science as Machinic Neoplatonism* (2017), *Counter Mapping the Smart City* (2017), and *Algorithmic Paranoia and the Convivial Alternative* (2016). McQuillan lives and works in London.

Johannes Paul Raether is an artist, holding a professorship for Artistic Practice in the Public Space at AdBK Nuremberg. Raether activates, feeds, and cares for several identities, or aLifveForms, which appear as humanoid beings in performative distributed social interventions, and operate as markers of constructed authorship and an evolutionary process of identity making and unmaking. The work of the aLifveForms explores questions of identity and reality in relation to language, and has been exhibited in solo and group exhibitions at Museum of Contemporary Art, Toronto (2019), Dortmunder Kunstverein (2019), and 6th Athens Bienniale (2018), among others. The aLifveForms have also made appearances at PACT, Essen (2019); BAK, basis voor actuele kunst, Utrecht (2019); Kampnagel, Hamburg (2018); Munich Kammerspiele (2018); and Stedelijk Museum Amsterdam (2017), among others. Raether lives and works in Berlin.

Natascha Sadr Haghighian is an artist whose work is primarily concerned with investigating the structural underpinnings and relationships of complicity between the respective complexes of politics, commerce, and industry, and in turn, their roles in dictating the shape and structure of mundane life. Sadr Haghighian creates solo and collaborative works in the fields of installation, performance, text, and sound. Sadr Haghighian is based in Berlin.

Andreas Siekmann is an artist whose work focuses on the processes of economization and power relations at display in public space. Recent solo exhibitions include *Falsche Freiheit | The Big Four*, Galerie Barbara Weiss, Berlin, 2017; *Andreas Siekmann – Aufzeichnungen aus einem postfaktischen Zeitalter*, LWL Museum für Kunst und Kultur, Münster, 2016; and *In the Stomach of the Predators* (with Alice Creischer), BAK, basis voor actuele kunst, Utrecht, 2014. Recent groups exhibitions include *. . . of bread, wine, cars, security and peace*, Kunsthalle Wien, 2020; and *Circular Flow*, Kunstmuseum Basel, 2019. Siekmann lives and works in Berlin.

Esmee Schoutens is a researcher and curator, currently working as Curator Public Program at Amsterdam Museum and Publications Officer at Stedelijk Museum Amsterdam. In her research as a masters student of Critical Studies in Art and Culture at Vrije Universiteit Amsterdam, Schoutens focused mostly on modern and contemporary art, specifically on art/technology collaborations and artistic responses to the rise of digital technology starting in the 1960s. Schoutens previously worked as manager and editor of *Stedelijk Studies* at the Stedelijk Museum Amsterdam and as editor for the magazine *Kunstlicht*. Schoutens works and lives in Amsterdam.

Jonas Staal is an artist and founder of the artistic and political organization New World Summit (2012–ongoing), the New World Academy (co-founded with BAK, basis voor actuele kunst, Utrecht, 2013–2016), and the New Unions campaign (2016–ongoing). Staal's interdisciplinary work includes interventions in public space, exhibitions, lectures, and publications that interrogate the relationship between art, democracy, ideology, politics, and propaganda. Recent publications include *Propaganda Art in the 21st Century* (2019), *Steve Bannon: A Propaganda Retrospective* (2018), and *Stateless Democracy* (edited with Renée In der Maur, in dialogue with the Kurdish Women's Movement, 2015). Recent projects include *Collectivize Facebook* (with Jan Fermon), HAU Hebbel am Ufer Berlin, Berlin, 2020; *Obscure Union* (with Laure Prouvost), Mercer Union, Toronto, 2019; *Training for the Future* (with Florian Malzacher), Ruhrtriennale, Bochum, 2019; and *redistribute toxicity* (with Jonas Stuck), SAVVY Contemporary—The Laboratory of Form-Ideas, Berlin, 2019. Staal lives and works in Rotterdam.

Acknowledgements

We thank all contributing artists, writers, and other practitioners involved in the realization of this reader, as well as the individuals and organizations listed below, who have contributed generously in a variety of ways to make this publication possible:

Guy Bonsiepe (Florianopolis), Filipa César (Berlin), Mitchell Esajas (Amsterdam), Galleria Continua (San Gimignano, Beijing, Les Moulins, Havana, and Rome), Galerie Krinzinger (Vienna), Galerie Nagel Draxler (Berlin, Cologne, and Munich), Jeanne van Heeswijk (Rotterdam), Victoria Hindley of MIT Press (Cambridge, MA), Grada Kilomba (Berlin), Marjolijn Kok (Amsterdam), Lehmann Maupin (Honk Kong, New York, and Seoul), Library of Congress (Washington, DC), Munchmuseet (Oslo), David Muñoz Alcántara (Helsinki), National Library of Norway (Oslo), Alejandro Navarrete (Utrecht), The Norwegian Labour Movements Archives and Library (Oslo), Oslo Museum (Oslo), Maria Pask (Amsterdam), Oleksiy Radynski (Kiev), Hélène des Rieux (Paris), Kamara Sassi (Paris), Whitney Stark (Amsterdam), Store Norkse Lexicon (Oslo), Valentina Vella (Utrecht), and VNS Matrix (Adelaide).

Diana McCarty wishes to thank Irene Calabuch Mirón, Maria Hlavajova, Sven Lütticken, Wietske Maas, Whitney Stark, and the team at BAK, basis voor actuele kunst, Utrecht.

The activities of BAK, basis voor actuele kunst have been made possible with financial support from Ministry of Education, Culture and Science, the Netherlands, and City Council, Utrecht.

Ministerie van Onderwijs, Cultuur en Wetenschap

Gemeente Utrecht

Index

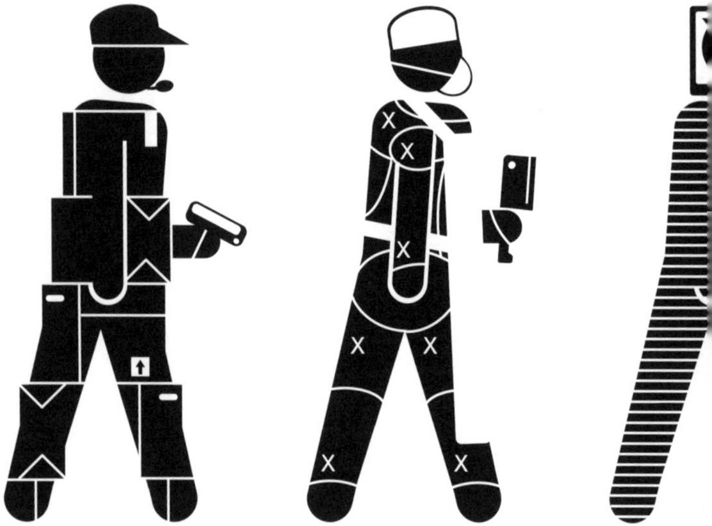

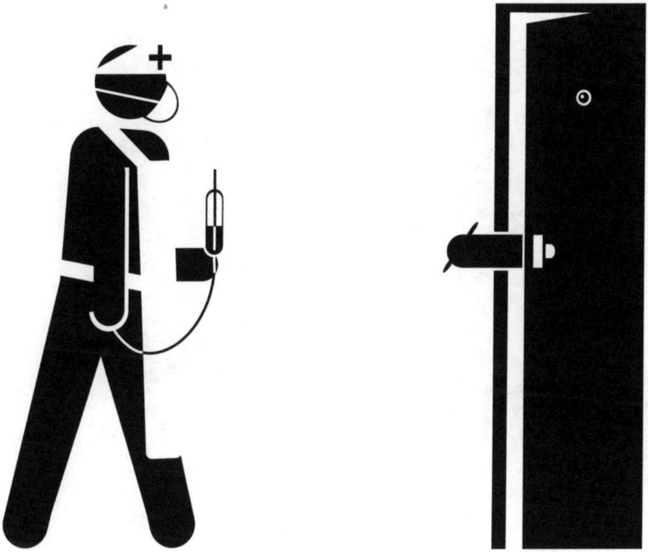

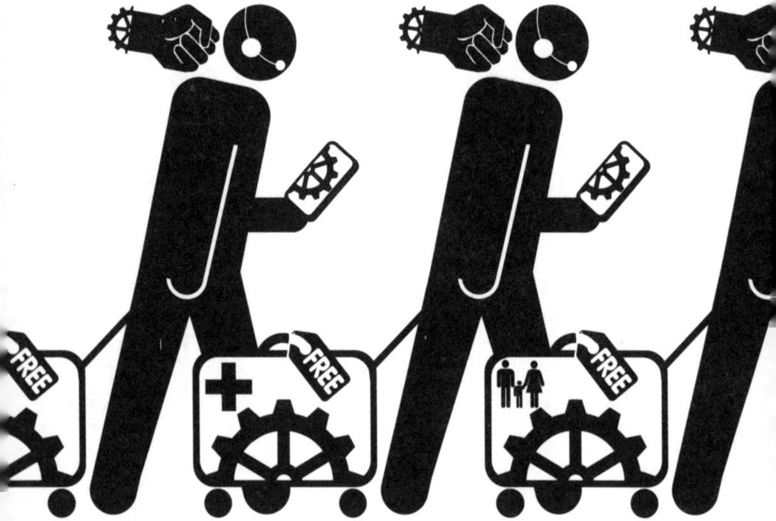
FREE
FREE
FREE

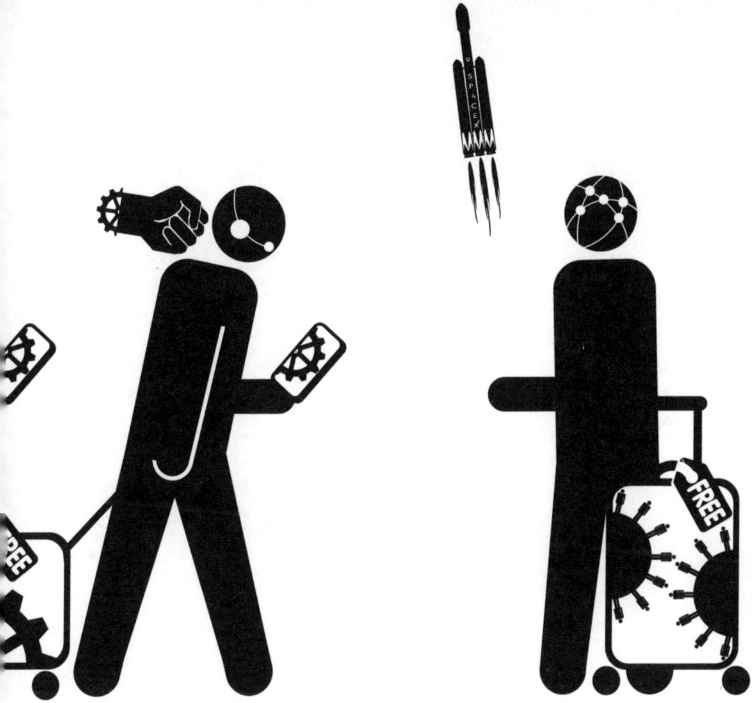

SPACEX
FREE